Talking About God When People Are Afraid

Dialogues on the Incarnation the Year That Doctor King and Senator Kennedy Were Killed

EDITED BY KEITH WATKINS
Foreword by Ronald J. Allen

WIPF & STOCK · Eugene, Oregon

TALKING ABOUT GOD WHEN PEOPLE ARE AFRAID
Dialogues on the Incarnation the Year That Doctor King and Senator Kennedy Were Killed

Copyright © 2020 Keith Watkins. All rights reserved. Except for brief quotations in critical publications or reviews, no part of this book may be reproduced in any manner without prior written permission from the publisher. Write: Permissions, Wipf and Stock Publishers, 199 W. 8th Ave., Suite 3, Eugene, OR 97401.

Revised Standard Version of the Bible, copyright 1952 [2nd edition, 1971] by the Division of Christian Education of the National Council of the Churches of Christ in the United States of America. Used by permission. All rights reserved.

Scripture quotations taken from the New English Bible, copyright © Cambridge University Press and Oxford University Press 1961, 1970. All rights reserved.

Wipf & Stock
An Imprint of Wipf and Stock Publishers
199 W. 8th Ave., Suite 3
Eugene, OR 97401

www.wipfandstock.com

PAPERBACK ISBN: 978-1-7252-7523-2
HARDCOVER ISBN: 978-1-7252-7524-9
EBOOK ISBN: 978-1-7252-7525-6

Manufactured in the U.S.A.   09/08/20

Talking About God
When People Are Afraid

We live, today, in an anxious world. Later generations will probably see our age as a time of transition from one social order to another, as we find the Middle Ages a "middle" between the Graeco-Roman civilization and the full-fledged European. But we cannot see the present that way, because what we are moving towards does not yet exist, and we can have no picture of it. Nor is the ascendancy of Europe— the concert of nations consisting of white people and their economic culture roughly coextensive with Christendom—as yet a finished act in history; but its form is broken. We feel ourselves swept along in a violent passage from a world we cannot salvage to one we cannot see, and most people are afraid.

SUSANNE K. LANGER, *PHILOSOPHICAL SKETCHES*

The Preachers

Robert A. Thomas, Senior Minister, University Christian Church, Seattle

Eugene Kidder, Minister of Youth and Pastoral Counseling, University Christian Church, Seattle

Thomas R. McCormick, Campus Minister, University of Washington, Seattle

Keith Watkins, Visiting Minister-Theologian, University Christian Church, 1967–1968, Professor of Worship and Parish Ministry, Christian Theological Seminary, Indianapolis

Contents

Foreword by Ronald J. Allen	ix
Acknowledgments	xv

An Experiment in Preaching

A Challenging Time to Preach about God	3
The Advent Dialogues	8
The Lenten Dialogues	12
Second Thoughts Two Generations Later	19
The Enduring Legacy	25

Advent Dialogues: Born to Set the People Free

Advent 1: Bound Robert A. Thomas	33
Advent 2: Doing Your Own Thing Thomas R. McCormick and Robert A. Thomas	39
Advent 3: Getting Your History Straight Eugene Kidder and Robert A. Thomas	48
Advent 4: Entering the Main Stream Keith Watkins and Robert A. Thomas	57
Advent 5: Delivered Robert A. Thomas	65

Lenten Dialogues:
The Tragic Vision

Lent 1: In Sight of the City He Wept *Robert A. Thomas*	75
Lent 2: His Hand with Mine on the Table *Keith Watkins and Robert A. Thomas*	81
Lent 3: In Anguish of Spirit He Prayed *Eugene Kidder and Robert A. Thomas*	90
Lent 4: His Teaching Is Causing Dissatisfaction *Thomas R. McCormick and Robert A. Thomas*	98

Lent 5: Do Not Weep for Me, Weep for Yourselves
   and Your Children
   Robert A. Thomas
	108

Lent 6: Why Search Among the Dead for One Who Lives? *Robert A. Thomas*	116
Bibliography	125

Foreword

The question might come up, "Why would a reader in the early twenty-first century be interested in sermons preached in 1967 and 1968?" The answer is that the 1960s were a period of unusual cultural ferment in North America, a ferment that included changes taking place in churches and in preaching, and we find ourselves in a similar situation as the 2020s unfold. Indeed, as I write in the spring of 2020, the United States is in the grip of the Covid-19 pandemic with its attendant social crises. The publication of the sermons in *Talking About God When People Are Afraid* opens a window into an important chapter in the history of preaching by demonstrating how preachers in the 1960s perceived and spoke about many of the existential issues and feelings facing people in the United States (especially in the Eurocentric, educated middle class). This window also prompts preachers more than fifty years later to consider how we might perceive and speak about culturally challenging issues today.

These sermons demonstrate how one group of preachers sought to help a congregation make theological sense of the force fields in the culture and the church and to imagine appropriate responses both as individuals and as a community of faith. Many sermons of the period of the late 1960s reflect similar emphases to the messages in this volume, but, in my view, the sermons here exemplify the best of that tradition in ways that surpass many other existing examples.

Foreword

Not only does the book open a window on the past, but it points towards some practices for preaching that can benefit the contemporary pulpit and church. Today's ministers cannot simply repeat what these preachers did a half-century ago, but we can draw inspiration for being as theologically responsible, pastorally sensitive, and sermonically creative as were the four preachers involved in these dialogues.

During the 1960s several great cultural forces swirled around one another in generating perceptions and feelings that were often in tension. On the one hand, these forces included the flourishing of science and technology which seemed to promise an ever-increasing good quality of life. The economy appeared to provide steady wages and benefits for many for both the present and the long-term future. There was a great emphasis on the "new"—new school buildings to accommodate growing enrollment, new church buildings to house congregations that had grown like wildfire in the previous decade, new shopping centers, new hospitals, even new and improved laundry detergents. General Electric used the slogan, "Progress is Our Most Important Product." There was a certain experimental feeling in the air as many people were open to doing things new ways.

On the other hand, the Cold War created anxiety that rubbed against this optimistic spirit. Many high school and college students and others responded to the Vietnam War by taking to the streets. Generational conflict was common especially between the World War II generation and their Boomer children. Hippies rejected many of the values and practices of corporate culture. Many young people who did not actually become hippies still looked upon aspects of the dominant culture with suspicion. The nation became freshly aware of the extent and depth of poverty. Anti-war protests in behalf of peace were sometimes accompanied by violence. Indeed, Martin Luther King Jr. was assassinated on April 4, 1968, and Robert F. Kennedy just two months later on June 5, 1968. Among people of color as well as among many Eurocentric people in solidarity with them, the Civil Rights Movement promised a better society even as that movement unnerved many Eurocentric communities.

Foreword

People in the 1960s were often simultaneously optimistic and anxious. It was a period of great creativity while also a time of contradiction and conflict. Preaching always partakes of the culture in which it is spoken, but the sermons in this volume especially do so. The preachers seek to help listeners make theological sense of the full range of the experience of the period from the standpoint of clear and cogent Christian vision. The sermons seek to interpret the interior experience of the individual as well as the more social dynamics of congregation and culture.

The sermons go back and forth between preaching that offers serious exposition of a biblical text in the traditional sermonic sense and those that are more topical in nature. In both cases, I am struck by the depth and precision of the preachers' understandings of the people and the culture of the time as well as the acuity of the preachers' theological analyses. These are points at which these sermons provide case studies for sermons today. To be candid, while many preachers today seek to interpret contemporary culture in theological perspective, the efforts seldom approach the substance of the sermons in *Talking About God When People Are Afraid*. I am further struck by the breadth and depth of learning that the preachers bring to the sermons. In addition to their own keen insights, the preachers draw on biblical scholarship, church history, systematic theology, ethics, ecumenical dialogue, philosophy, and psychology to extents that are rarely reached in preaching today. In these regards, the early twenty-first-century pulpit could take clues from these sermons.

As the title of the volume implies, one of the most distinctive aspects of the sermons is their dialogical character. After World War II, the biblical scholar Hans Conzelmann commented that the impetus for Redaction Criticism to Form Criticism as a primary approach to interpreting the Bible was just "in the air." Something of the same is true for the notion of dialogue in the 1960s, symbolized, perhaps, by the 1963 publication of Reuel L. Howe, *The Miracle of Dialogue*. Howe—an Episcopal priest, former faculty member at a theological seminary, and founder of the Institute for Advanced Pastoral Studies in Bloomfield, Michigan—symbolized the wider presence of dialogue as a force-field in the culture while he also

Foreword

contributed to that presence by reinforcing the notion that dialogue is central to developing authentic relationships and community.[1]

In the 1960s, Christian education increasingly moved away from top-down, information-based approaches and more towards discussion and dialogue. This emphasis appeared in other forms of ecclesial life but was slow to come to the pulpit. *Dialogues on the Incarnation* is a pioneering effort to bring the spirit of dialogue to the pulpit. Most of the sermons feature interchanges between Robert A. Thomas, Senior Minister of the congregation, and a second person—Associate Minister Eugene Kidder, Campus Minister Thomas R. McCormick, or Keith Watkins, a member of the faculty of Christian Theological Seminary who was Visiting Minister Theologian for the academic year 1967–68. Thomas preaches in a solo voice in the first sermons in the series for Advent and Lent and also in the last sermon of each series. His solo-voice sermons are not singular, isolated messages but are intended to introduce the dialogue that takes place not only in the individual sermons but in the messages interacting with one another for the whole of each season. His solo voice at the end is a kind of wrap-up or summary.

Most of the time, the interaction between Thomas and the other preacher for the day has the character of real dialogue, that is, give-and-take, question and response, question prompting question, or affirmation prompting expansion. Listeners have a sense of the sermon moving in the same way that conversations move. At some other times, to be honest, the content of the sermon, while expressed in two voices, is a single line of thought that could be spoken by a single voice without loss of meaning. This slight inconsistency does not detract from the innovative quality of the dialogical approach.

Between the 1960s and today, scholarship in preaching has given almost no attention to the possibility of genuine give-and-take between two voices (or among more voices) in the sermon.[2] I

---

1. Howe, *Miracle of Dialogue.*

2. A movement in scholarship in preaching under the heading of "conversational preaching" does envision the sermon as having the characteristics of a conversation in its search for an adequate interpretation of God's presence and purposes. However, the authors in this field envision much conversational

Foreword

am aware of only a few isolated instances of such preaching, often on the part of clergy couples.

However, the early twenty-first century is an ideal time in which to reclaim the kind of multiple-voice preaching demonstrated in *Talking About God When People Are Afraid*. We are at a cultural moment in which many Eurocentric peoples are rediscovering community. Congregations with multiple ministers—on the staff or containing ministers who are simply members—can easily take advantage of the multiple ministerial presence for dialogical preaching.

Going further, one of the important themes in the emerging postmodern culture in both the wider world and in theology and the church is boundary-crossing, or transgression. While the expert is still respected, there is a growing sense that experts often have limited perspectives, and that people outside of expert status often have important things to contribute to discussion. From this point of view, ministers should no longer think of themselves as *the* sources of theological insight for preaching. Indeed, increasing numbers of clergy are making use of sermon feed-forward groups in which ministers meet with lay people as part of sermon preparation.[3] It is a short small step from clergy and laity thinking together about the sermon in the study to clergy and laity speaking with one another in the pulpit.

To be sure, everything in this volume should not be a spark for preaching in the present. Most of these sermons lasted about half an hour—one or two perhaps as long as forty minutes. Few congregations in the historic denominations today are prepared to make this kind of investment in the sermon. Moreover, the sermons are written in a style that is as much literary as oral-aural. Indeed, some of the sermons are almost essay-like style in a way that would sound stilted in the pulpit today. While the sermons are exceptional

---

preaching as conversational in spirit and theological perspective but monological in expression from the pulpit. The single voice of the preacher leads the congregation in a conversation about the ideas important to the sermon e.g., Allen, *The Homiletic of All Believers*; Allen and Allen, *The Sermon Without End*.

3. The classic work is McClure, *The Roundtable Pulpit*. Cf. Howe, *Partners in Preaching*.

Foreword

in theological penetration, the preachers seldom address listeners directly, in the way that would be typical of active dialogue today. Indeed, I am struck by how often the sermons are almost third-person in their rhetorical orientation.

Moreover, the preachers do not make use of many stories to help the sermons come alive and to help listeners connect the big ideas of their sermon. The preacher today wants to make greater use of narrative. To make an obvious point: these observations reinforce the value of the volume as a resource for the study of the history of preaching. While we can learn things to do from these messages, we can also note qualities that are better adapted. In both cases, *Talking About God When People Are Afraid* is an excellent resource for the preacher today.

RONALD J. ALLEN
Professor of Preaching, and Gospels and Letters, Emeritus
Christian Theological Seminary

Acknowledgments

I am grateful to Tom McCormick for the extended conversations about University Christian Church that we shared while this book was taking shape. Because his ministry at the University of Washington and his membership in University Christian Church have continued throughout the half century since we participated in this "experiment in preaching," his insights and encouragement gave me the sense of freedom to continue the project. At a later stage, Judy Thomas Christianson and Paul E. Kidder, who were youth in the church when we preached these sermons, responded positively to my publishing these examples of their fathers' work.

Even more, I have depended upon my daughter, Marilyn P. Watkins, who was in the sixth grade during the year that we lived in Seattle. Following graduation from college, she established her permanent home in Seattle and except for the years when she was doing PhD studies at the University of Michigan has lived in Seattle ever since. She and her late husband, Cy Ulberg, were active members of University Christian Church and this was the congregation where their family received their spiritual nurture. When visiting her through the years, I have attended worship with her and thus continued my association with the gradually diminishing number of people who heard these sermons so many years ago.

Marilyn and I have often talked about Seattle, especially the University District, and about the ministry of her church in this community. She has helped me understand the changes that have taken place during more than five decades of passing time. Her

Acknowledgments

comments were especially helpful as I drafted the essay that introduces this "experiment in preaching." Her work for many years as policy director for the Economic Opportunity Institute in Seattle is in its own way an expression of values exemplified by University Christian Church and affirmed in sermons such as those in these *Dialogues on the Incarnation*.

Soon after completing the transcription of these sermons and drafting an essay describing the context within which we had performed our "experiment in preaching," I asked my colleague and friend, Ronald J. Allen, to read them and offer his comments. He encouraged me to complete the project and seek publication, and he has advised me along the way. I am grateful for his support in the publishing process and his willingness to write the Foreword which sets forth so clearly the reasons why these sermons from long ago deserve to have a continuing life.

During that tumultuous year in Seattle I wrote a book entitled *Liturgies in a Time When Cities Burn* (Abingdon, 1969). The statement I used in my dedication holds true even now: To the members and staff of University Christian Church, Seattle, 1967–68, and especially Robert A. Thomas: "I was a stranger and you welcomed me."

An Experiment in Preaching

A Challenging Time to Preach about God

Early in the evening of April 4, 1968, Doctor Martin Luther King Jr., thirty-nine years of age, was shot and killed in Memphis. A short time later that same day, Senator Robert F. Kennedy consoled a mostly black assemblage in Indianapolis who only then were hearing the tragic news. Two months later, on the evening of June 5, Senator Kennedy was shot at the Ambassador Hotel in Los Angeles after winning the California presidential primary. He died the next day. These murders were but two of the fear-inspiring events during one of the most tragic years in American history.

During those tumultuous months, I was in Seattle, serving as visiting minister-theologian at University Christian Church (Disciples of Christ). Living, working, and ministering in this vibrant, complex, controversial, and liberal university community was a life-shaping experience for me. At the close of the academic year 1967–68, significantly changed, I returned to my faculty position at Christian Theological Seminary in Indianapolis.

Everything I did that year was shaped by the challenge of presenting the Christian gospel to the increasingly skeptical, irreligious, anti-war, and hippie constituencies who seemed to dominate the University District where I spent most of my working hours. Questions were easy to state. Who is Jesus? What is his relationship with God? And what about God? What good is a God in heaven when the world that this God supposedly created and cares for is in such a mess? What does the church, with its quaint ideas and fussy ceremonies, have to do with anything, anyway? After church on the Sunday following Dr. King's death, a black barber made the question personal when he asked me: "Now, professor, what can we do to keep people from smashing my windows still another time?"

These issues consumed the mind, heart, and work of Robert A. Thomas, senior minister of the church. In his sermons week after week he dealt seriously with conditions in the world and proclaimed the relevance of the Christian faith to a world that seemed to be falling apart. I had never heard preaching like this before. His liberal theology had been formed during his studies in the Divinity School at the University of Chicago, one of the nation's most prestigious and influential seminaries. He believed that science, history, and the Christian faith could live together and that insights drawn from these streams of thought could be united in our efforts to resolve the social and personal crises of human life and society.

Bob wrote his sermons in serious, declarative prose, long sentences, complete with dependent clauses. He included quotations from the Bible, scholars old and new, and current news sources, convinced that in an academic community, sermons had to be intellectually persuasive.

Standing tall in the high pulpit, dressed in his black academic gown with wide sleeves, he read the sermons word for word, with full voice and animated style, his arms flailing the air. Week after week, I felt a rising tide of excitement as sermon time drew near.

Midway through the fall season, Bob invited three of his clergy colleagues to join him in planning and preaching a series of dialogue sermons during the Advent Season that would begin a few weeks later. One other member of the ministerial staff, Mary Elizabeth Mason, was not invited to be part of the team even though she was a seminary graduate and previously had headed one of the divisions of the denomination's United Christian Missionary Society based in Indianapolis. Even in liberal congregations like University Christian Church, women were not yet allowed to serve as elders, and it was rare for a woman's voice to be heard from the pulpit.

Bob proposed that we choose a theme rooted in the Christmas story and relevant to the tempestuous world in which we lived and

A Challenging Time to Preach about God

then preach a series of dialogue sermons. Although the writings of Reuel Howe[1] had popularized a dialogic approach to preaching, Bob had his own ideas about how the four of us would work together, and in the first sermon of the series he explained this understanding of dialogue to the congregation. These sermons would be "the product (in some ways, at least) of all our minds in dialogue." They were not "some kind of phony "conversation" but, instead, carefully prepared and scripted proclamations of the gospel. We called them dialogue sermons, but a better term might have been collegial sermons because four colleagues fully shared the responsibility for shaping, delivering, and evaluating these pastoral addresses.

We met two or three times to develop the format for the series, select the topics that the five sermons would proclaim, and assign the preachers. Bob and his dialogue partner would then prepare a sermon, in full manuscript, and preach it. Each week the four of us would evaluate the sermon just preached and discuss ideas that might go into the next Sunday's sermon. We invited the religion editor of one of the Seattle newspapers to join us for one or two of our weekly planning sessions. There was no question about who was senior partner in this collegial relationship. Bob was several years older than the rest of us, and he was pastor of the church, the one who carried primary responsibility for worship, preaching, and congregational well-being. His was the single voice in two of the five sermons.

We agreed that Bob would begin the series on November 26, the Sunday between Thanksgiving and the beginning of Advent. He would explain the experiment, announce the theme, and describe the challenges of our time that we believed the Christian gospel could help to overcome. During each of the next three weeks, Bob and one of the younger clergy would describe one aspect of our human condition and point toward the Christ-centered response that the Christmas story offers. On the last Sunday of Advent, which that year was December 24, Christmas Eve, Bob would in his morning sermon proclaim the miracle of new life that Jesus brings to

---

1. Two books by Reuel L. Howe were stimulating this discussion: *The Miracle of Dialogue*, published in 1963, had initiated the conversation and *Partners in Preaching*, published in 1967, had moved it forward.

the world. Although this sermon concluded our series, we knew that the liturgical climax would come that evening. An hour before midnight, a vast assemblage crowded into the large sanctuary. Sitting in the balcony with our children, I was overwhelmed by the beauty and spiritual power of the choir, with my wife in the alto section, as it processed through the church singing Benjamin Britten's *A Ceremony of Carols*. The celebration of the birth of Jesus and candlelight communion expressed a deep sense of joy and wonder.

Developing and preaching these sermons was exhilarating for the four of us and well-received by the congregation, enough so that early in the new year, we decided to do it again on the Sundays in Lent, beginning March 3, 1968, and culminating on Easter Sunday, April 14. We gave titles to these series: Advent: *Born to Set the People Free*; Lent: *The Tragic Vision*; and the two sets combined: *Dialogues on the Incarnation*.

Walter Hansen, the church's business manager, typed the scripts for us each Sunday, and a carbon-copy set has been tucked away in my files these many years. As part of my remembrance, fifty years later, of that tragic year in American life, I transcribed these sermons— all thirty thousand words—and reflected upon the gospel that four preachers in the U District of Seattle proclaimed in a time when the world was in turmoil.

During that year in Seattle, I was reading steadily in a wide range of theologically oriented writings in scholarly monographs and journals of opinion, giving special attention to Ernst Cassirer's philosophy of symbolic forms and Susanne Langer's writings on the philosophy of artistic expression. It was one of the most fruitful periods of my life as professor of worship and pastoral work. As the year drew to a close, I wrote a book—still my favorite of the ten that I have published—that was based on the year's research and my serious conversations with church people: its title, *Liturgies in a Time When Cities Burn*. As frontispiece, I used a paragraph from one of Susanne Langer's books in which she wrote that we are living in an anxious world that is going through "a transition from one social order to another." Although the old order is still with us, "its form is broken," and we cannot yet see what the future will be. "We feel ourselves swept along in a violent passage, from a world we cannot salvage to one we cannot see; and most people are afraid."[2]

Half a century later, those words are still true. The old order seems even more precarious now than ever. We have little sense of what is still to come. Langer's words, that "most people are afraid," continue to be true. It may be that people today are even more anxious about the future than we were half a century ago when these sermons were preached. The dialogic pattern and the homiletical style we used were uniquely designed for that time and place. The specific issues we addressed differed in detail from those that confront us now as the world rushes wildly through the early years of the twenty-first century. Preachers today will probably modify the dialogical form we used as they seek to deliver the good news. Despite these differences, we can take confidence in the conviction that "Jesus Christ is the same yesterday and today and forever" (Heb 13:8).

---

2. Langer, *Philosophical Sketches*. See especially pages 95–106, 123–52.

The Advent Dialogues

The five sermons in the Advent series read like the chapters of a short book. In the first sermon, "Bound," Robert Thomas described the human condition. Most people come into the world bound by "internal mechanisms of control," including emotional conflicts, physical drives, and motivations. We are surrounded by crime and environmental conditions over which we have no control, by governmental actions, and by the routines of daily life. In the final paragraph of the sermon, he turned the corner by asking the question: "What has the incarnation to do with this? Does Christ come yet to set the people free?" In two sentences, he declared the answer. "That is our faith; that in the midst of the life of the world—this world of business and organization and specialization and conformities and institutions and fear of death and unconscious powers and motivations—Christ comes. He brings liberty to the captives and the opening of the prison to those who are bound." In these final sentences, he told the congregation how the series would end, but he intimated that the full narrative would be revealed week by week in the sermons still to come. The next three sermons were to explore ways that people of that time were trying, unsuccessfully, to escape from their condition of being bound to a new life of freedom. Then would come the sermon that proclaimed deliverance.

In the second Advent sermon, Thomas McCormick, campus minister at the University of Washington's main campus, described one way that some people were using to escape the bondage that had been described the previous Sunday. Using the abundant hippie

The Advent Dialogues

community as the chief example, he described how people were dropping out in response to personal experiences, such as absentee fathers, and political issues, especially the Vietnam War and nuclear weapons. Their plan of action was to "hang loose." He reminded the congregation that many people who still live conventional lives harbored secret desires to join the hippies.

Thomas then asked the question that these sermons were intended to answer: "What does the incarnation have to do with all of this?" The answer that he and McCormick gave was that hanging loose was not the kind of freedom that we really want. Thomas quoted an entry that Dag Hammarskjöld, secretary-general of the United Nations, had written in his journal in 1961. At a certain moment in his life, he had answered "Yes to Someone—or Something—and from that hour I was certain that existence is meaningful and that, therefore, my life, in self-surrender, had a goal. From that moment I have known what it means 'not to look back,' and 'to take no thought for the morrow.'"[1]

Thomas concluded the sermon with one of his characteristically long sentences: "That is the freedom that comes, not in isolation, not in dropping out, not in disconnection from tradition, not in irresponsibly 'doing your own thing,' but only through getting your history straight, and in commitment, response, and self-surrender to the God who makes himself known in Jesus Christ—'the man for others' who was 'born to set the people free.'"

The third sermon in the Advent series explored one of the phrases in that sentence, "getting your history straight." Joining Thomas on this Sunday was Eugene Kidder, associate minister of the congregation, who devoted much of his time to pastoral counseling with members of the congregation and many others from the larger community. Thomas began the conversation by asking if people really wanted to be free and Kidder answered, "Yes." We were created with this desire and when we feel bound, we try to break loose. Forty percent of the people seeking help, he noted, come first to a minister. "They come as nomads in search of the selves they've never found, or lost, or left behind." Many come "bearing on their

---

1. Hammarskjöld, *Markings*, 205.

backs the burdens of generations before them." When they find help they are afraid—afraid that they are "destined to repeat the failures of the generations before them."

Thomas responded that "the biblical view of history is linear" rather than cyclical. The cycles from the past are to be broken so that people can live forward into new lives. Agreeing, Kidder added that this new life is most fully possible with a counselor and with other people in "a supportive community with a common faith." Concluding the sermon, Thomas again declared the central theme of the entire series. "Life in such a community of faith is daily experience of death, burial, and resurrection. It is creative encounter with God, self, and others that leads to 'getting our history straight—recovering the meaning of the past, living joyfully in the present, and being hopefully expectant of the future.' And possible at all because One was 'born to set the people free.'"

Thomas began the fourth Advent sermon, in which I was the dialogue partner, by quoting a member of Congress who described the tiredness, frustration, and uneasiness that marked the mood on Capitol Hill. He continued by again quoting Susanne Langer's assertion, that most people are afraid. Referring to the previous Sunday's sermon which affirmed that we need to get our personal histories straight, he broadened the theme with the assertion that we need to understand "our Tradition as people in the Western world" and see "ourselves as part of an ongoing process that is at the same time conserving and creative."

In my response, I pointed to efforts from within the academy and the church (including the "old guard" of every congregation of every denomination) to stifle new life. Together Thomas and I sought to distinguish between Tradition with a capital T and traditions with a lower-case t. We affirmed that the "Christian Tradition is a vision of meaning in the face of absurdity, a conviction of purpose in the natural order seemingly devoid of reason, a certainty that individual life makes sense despite the despair that so easily besets us."

Near the conclusion of the sermon, Thomas declared that in our time "when an upheaval in history is occurring that seems more drastic than anything people have known before, when no one can see a picture of what the future will be, our need is for awareness of the reality of the deep-running stream of Tradition made known in the work of Jesus Christ in the world."

Just as the first sermon of the series was devoted to an exposition of being "Bound," so in the last Advent sermon Thomas described and affirmed the "Deliverance" that Christians celebrate in the incarnation of Jesus whose birth is celebrated at this time of the year. Again, he declared that people everywhere long for freedom from all that holds them in some kind of imprisonment. "The hope of salvation, of deliverance, in one form or another, has always been part of religion, and when there has seemed no basis for hope for worldly well-being, men and women have sought 'a salvation not made with hands' from some realm beyond earthly existence." He noted that there are two kinds of religion—religions of escape and religions of liberation. Both tendencies, he continued, have been present in the history of the church, but the dominant note throughout the Jewish and Christian traditions has been liberation. He drew upon the biblical record—from Jeremiah, Joel, Luke, and John—to support this interpretation of the Christian faith. Once again, his final paragraph drove the point home.

"Deliverance in our experience comes through the effort, suffering, and devotion of persons, but in the larger sense that deliverance always comes from God. The suffering of God is not finished. The labor of God is not done. We are being delivered from the prisons of darkness and fear and death to become free persons, loving human beings, living in communities of love. The God of Abraham, Isaac, and Jacob is the God of Jesus Christ, is the God of the people of this time, and is the God of the future that is to be. We have been bound, but we are being delivered by One 'born to set the people free!'"

The Lenten Dialogues

Following the pattern established in the Advent series of sermons, Robert Thomas devoted the first Lenten sermon to the theme that he and his three colleagues intended to develop during the following season. He stated that at a time when many peoples' reflections alternate "between consideration of events in Christ's life and events in our own" the Scripture readings and the sermons would "encourage introspection in the light of the gospel of the crucified and risen Lord." He referred to recent "gospels of modernity" and their teachings that science or education could resolve the problems of life. In contrast, he continued, poets, dramatists, disillusioned philosophers, other writers, and theologians were "making common cause against the sentimentality of former generations, vigorously attacking that delusive optimism which held that goodness always triumphs." After citing disorders of the time—urban crisis, the Vietnam war, and hordes of refugees—he referred to Nathan Scott's 1957 book, *The Tragic Vision and the Christian Faith*, declaring that all of us are displaced persons "who cannot find anywhere a satisfactory dwelling place in the world of our time."

Acknowledging that "the final accent of the Christian proclamation is *not* on tragedy, but on hope and victory," he declared that this hope depends, in part, upon our facing seriously "the passion of Jesus, the pain and anguish of our Lord, its evidence of the God who himself suffers and thereby accomplishes our deliverance." Thomas described Jesus' final trip to Jerusalem as the turning point of his life's work and the beginning of a series of events that would result in his crucifixion a few days later. It would be his final effort to persuade his followers and the crowds that his mission was religious, not political. Jesus came proclaiming the coming of the kingdom of God, but his disciples and the crowds did not understand his message or realize that he faced the probability of death. He wept tears of tragedy, not for himself, but for them. The sermon concluded with a declaration that God sees the cities of our time much as Jesus saw Jerusalem, as places marked by materialism, destructive forces, and suffering. "Christ still weeps, and still hopes, and God still intends the Kingdom."

The second Lenten sermon, "His Hand with Mine on the Table," developed one of the factors that helped to account for the tragedy described in the introductory sermon: the conflict between two powerful forces that have always been present in human life. The more obvious of the two is the "will to achieve, to become a success, to gain wealth and power, to seek one's 'place in the sun.'" The other powerful force is clearly seen in Jesus "who went about 'doing good,' who seemed to care little for his own physical needs and advised his disciples to give their attention to other matters first."

As the dialogue partner in this sermon, I summarized the history of Israel, beginning with David's reign, and pointed to the contrast between "the kingly messiah" who would lead the Jewish people to military victory and political power and "the Suffering Servant" who would be "despised and rejected by the people, a man of sorrows, and acquainted with grief, wounded, bruised, oppressed, rejected—and all for the sake of the people whom he came to serve but who turned away from him."

At Jesus' Last Supper with his disciples, this conflict and the seemingly inevitable tragedy that would soon occur were the dominant factors in his heart and mind. During the meal's ceremonies with bread and wine, Jesus added a new meaning when he declared that this broken bread was his body. I then referred to "two elements—disaster and hope—that must be present for an event to be tragic," and supported this idea with references to contemporary writer Charles G. Bell[1] and classic authors, Shakespeare and Ibsen.

---

1. Bell, "Tragedy," 12–32.

Both factors were present as Jesus and his closest friends participated in that last meal together.

Thomas concluded the sermon by asserting that at the table "the Suffering Servant confronts his disciples, and those who are considering discipleship, with the fundamental choice as to life's dominant motif—whether or not it will be the servant stance for us. The crisis of his decision is reconstituted in this room, his hand with ours on the table, his life calling ours to the way of servanthood." On this Sunday the liturgical force of the sermon-sacramental supper sequence was especially clear. The word proclaimed brought worshipers to the table where we encountered once again the Word made flesh (see John 1:14).

Eugene Kidder and Robert Thomas devoted the third Lenten sermon, "In Anguish of Spirit, He Prayed," to what happened in the garden of Gethsemane where Jesus and his disciples went to pray after finishing their somber meal. "Gethsemane closes the door on any spiritualizing of Jesus or our faith in him," Kidder stated. "No more human picture of him is found in the New Testament. The valiancy of his work of mission and the agony of his suffering were so bound together in Jesus as to be almost indistinguishable. In Gethsemane these realities were expanded to ultimate proportions and Jesus was stretched to the breaking point. That event, written upon the face of history, epitomizes the deepest suffering of all who live in the spirit."

As they concluded the sermon, both preachers referred to the sleeping disciples, and to other followers who were not there, who seemed to have abandoned Jesus in the hour of his deepest grief. All that can be said of them was "that they misunderstood who he was and the nature of his mission; only that they failed him when he needed them most." Kidder then spoke in their defense. Soon thereafter, they experienced the resurrection and were the first to proclaim the good news. They carried the gospel across land and sea, and they organized the church. Thomas continued the recitation of their good work after the resurrection and concluded: "So anguish may turn to acceptance, and failure of discipleship may be the prelude to commitment, and the purposes of God redeemed from the worst work of the enemies of the Son of Man."

The Lenten Dialogues

In the fourth sermon of the Lenten series, "His Teaching Is Causing Disaffection," Thomas McCormick and Robert Thomas interpreted the scriptural accounts of the public trials that came next in the narrative of those fateful hours. As had been done in earlier sermons, they acknowledged that the biblical narratives differed in detail, but then identified what seemed to them to be the heart of the message. Both Jewish and Roman authorities were agreed: "His teaching is causing disaffection among the people all through Judea. It started from Galilee and has spread as far as this city" (Luke 23:5).

Thomas explained: "Disaffection is a strong word, describing a condition that autocrats in every age and place fear. It means an alienation from those in authority; at least a lack of affection or good will; at most a tendency toward hostility and ill will. From the point of view of those interested in protecting the status quo, maintaining the establishment, carrying on in the traditional ways, the disaffected are disloyal and apt to be dangerous or traitorous. They are the dangerous nonconformists who must be silenced or destroyed." The two preachers alternated in illustrating ways that political and religious leaders are threatened in tragic periods of time. McCormick then referred to Christopher Frye's description of Greek tragedy as "the catastrophe which occurs when the individual's vision or value conflicts with the structures of society."

In his conclusion, Thomas told the congregation that one reason for "struggles in the church of our time is the new insistence of its most committed leaders and members that the faith relate to the life of the world, that the church speak and act as its Lord, that it really become a servant people, that it turn from its temptation to accept the judgments of the world about its life and work and test its life and work by the revealing Word of God alone."

The fifth sermon in the Lenten series bears the title "Do Not Weep for Me, Weep for Yourselves and Your Children." Thomas reminded the congregation that the purpose of the Lenten series had been "to discover in the major events in the last period of Jesus' life the meanings that are significant for our time in the world's history.... Our commitment is to the living God, made known in the Christ-event; not only in an age long past, but in this nation now." After summarizing evidences of "growing frustration" throughout the nation, he declared that there was "lack of leadership to foster change and unwillingness on the part of the majority to make the sacrifices necessary to the achievement of justice. It is in this kind of world, he continued, "where the skein of tragedy is woven through the texture of man's life, that we have to measure the meaning and significance of Jesus' life, answer the questions about the nature of Ultimate Reality, and make the fundamental choices and commitments regarding our own lives."

Thomas devoted the central portion of the sermon to a description of the cruel character of Jesus' final hours and his intense suffering. He stressed the fact that neither the gospel writers nor Jesus himself emphasized the physical suffering. The center of what they remembered and proclaimed was "a precise recollection of his spiritual agony, the sense of being abandoned by God. They did not seek pity for Jesus and made it clear he did not seek it for himself." He wept because the people whom he came to lead toward a new way of living "in the kingdom's cause" would not change "from the pursuit of pleasure or material things or nationalistic glory in true repentance to the God of love and grace." In a long paragraph, Thomas listed the many tragic circumstances of life in the world right then and concluded this recitation. "We weep for all the destructiveness and inability to come to grips with reality that is around us [and] for all the tragic limitations and failures that keep the world from becoming the kingdom of God's love."

On Thursday evening of that week—Maundy Thursday, April 4, 1968—Dr. Martin Luther King Jr. was assassinated in Memphis, Tennessee. Three days later, the congregation gathered to celebrate Palm Sunday. The service for that day had already been planned to feature Cantata No. 4 by J. S. Bach, "Christ Lay in Death's Dark Prison," sung by the church's choir with organ and orchestra, to take the place of the sermon. Instead of listening to the gospel word proclaimed from the pulpit, the congregation joined the choir in singing stanzas one and seven of the final hymn in the cantata (with the choir singing stanzas two through six). By singing these words, the worshipers became immediate participants in that day's dialogue on the incarnation.

Christ lay by death enshrouded, from mortal sin to save us;
He is again arisen, Eternal life he gave us.
So now let us joyful be, and magnify him thankfully. Hallelujah!

To celebrate this Holy Feast in reverence united.
The evil leaven works no more. Thy Word its curse has righted.
Christ himself the Feast will be and nourish our souls
That we by faith may gain salvation. Hallelujah!

On Easter Sunday, the final challenge for the Lenten series of sermons was to proclaim the message of new life in a manner convincing enough to counteract the somber character of the five sermons that had explored the many-faceted suffering that Jesus experienced during his final week. The tragedy of Jesus' death and burial had an epilogue, Thomas declared to his congregation. The disciples emerged from hiding, rejoicing in a mighty faith and new hope, and started a movement that "laid hold of multitudes and . . . affected the transformation of human hearts" around the world. The one explanation that seemed adequate was the one given in Acts 2:24. "God raised him to life again, setting him free from the pangs of death, because it could not be that death should keep him in its grip." In answer to the idea that the accounts of resurrection were illusion or deliberate deception, he quoted Jesus scholar Joseph Klausner: "It is impossible to suppose that there was any conscious deception: the nineteen hundred years' faith of millions is not founded on deception."

The question that Thomas faced was how the people of our time were to understand the resurrection. Part of his answer was to call attention to the inconsistencies and problems in the gospel record itself, which enabled him to state that in the disciples' time and in ours *"the resurrection faith must be distinguished from the gospel stories about it."* After noting variant ideas in biblical writings, including those of Paul and concluding with John, he concluded: "Jesus had come back to trusting hearts as the Holy Spirit, the Comforter, the Helper, the Counselor, guiding them into the full truth." The idea that "Jesus' resurrection was a physical re-animation played only a very brief role in the serious thinking of the ancient church." Instead, it was an idea declared in the First Epistle of John, describing "this return as an inward, spiritual force that proved to be indominable."

Referring to the conclusion reached by one of "the great modern historians of the church," Thomas declared that there "can be no doubt that Christians through the ages have been honest in reporting an experience of 'being with a Presence' associated with the historical Jesus." He called attention to Martin Luther King Jr. as an example of a person whose life and ministry were sustained by this faith. "What we declare in this terrible time," Thomas continued, "is that the emancipating event has occurred; that Christ has infinite significance both for the individual destiny and for the future of the human race." In answer to many who during the past ten days had been asking if life can have any meaning, Thomas concluded the sermon with a paragraph, delivered with the full force of his personal and rhetorical power.

"That is our faith; that is our testimony this Easter day. We are not alone in an uncaring universe—alone with our sins and follies, our loss and grief and pain, our guns with telescopic sights, our unbridled hates and unreasonable judgments, our racism and nuclear power, our divided church with its traditional forms and reluctance to serve in the world. We are in the hands of God and God is the one 'who raised Christ Jesus from the dead.'"

Second Thoughts
Two Generations Later

As an every-Sunday church goer, I have listened to more than two thousand sermons since the four of us preached "Dialogues on the Incarnation" in 1967–68. In all these years I have neither seen nor heard other sermons similar to them in manner of development or content. Robert Thomas was right when he said that we were "engaged in an experiment in preaching." We received positive and reaffirming responses from people in the congregation, which gave us more reason to believe that the experiment had gone well. Even if we had wanted to build upon this pattern of preaching, our team soon separated so that we could not reconvene to develop another set of dialogues.

Early in June of that year, I returned to my continuing work as professor of worship and pastoral work at Christian Theological Seminary in Indianapolis. Later in 1968, Eugene Kidder left the staff in order to cofound and direct the Pastoral Institute of Washington. In 1972, he and his wife Barbara Kidder established a private practice in counseling. Thomas McCormick's primary work was as campus minister, and he soon was appointed to a faculty position at the University of Washington. In 1973, Robert Thomas was invited to become the president of the Board of Overseas Ministries of the Christian Church (Disciples of Christ), one of the most challenging leadership positions that our church offered. Moving to Indianapolis, he enlarged his focus to include the whole world. It seems clear to me, as I look back upon these dialogical sermons, that they were possible because of a unique and brief coming together of a particular group of preachers in a highly distinctive community and church.

Half a century after we delivered these dialogues, I have been rereading them and in keeping with my longtime habits have written evaluative comments. Although these dialogues were shaped by unique circumstances, it still is appropriate to evaluate them according to broader and continuing criteria of sermonic form. I have been guided, in part, by two publications of Ronald E. Osborn, a church historian with a life-long interest in preaching. In a technical essay published eight years after the Seattle Dialogues had been preached, Osborn defined Christian preaching and proposed "a tool" for evaluating sermons. Preaching, he wrote, is intended "to evoke faith in the spiritual reality professed by the believing congregation [and] to bring a recognition and repudiation of wrong." Most hearers "already believe, at least to a degree; with regard to them the purpose is confirmation and intensification of the faith they already have. . . . The preaching of the Bible 'demands our decision, our selves.'"[1] Bringing our hearers face to face with the demands and promises of Scripture was very much a part of our hope for these dialogues.

This living engagement with the Bible took place, I believe, even though these sermons were less explicit in their biblical connections than I now believe they should have been. The Advent series is a thoroughgoing example of what literature about preaching calls topical preaching. The topic itself, rather than a specific biblical text, controlled the development of ideas and identified the relevance these ideas have for living faithfully in the modern world. References to the Bible were used sparingly, primarily to illustrate or confirm ideas in the sermon. While there was a strong congruence between the ideas in the sermons we preached during Advent and ideas in the Bible, it seems clear to me now that the Bible itself was incidental to the development of these messages.

---

1. Osborn, "A Functional Definition of Preaching," 53–72. The quoted paragraph is on 68.

In contrast, the Lenten series used the Bible more prominently. Each of these sermons selected a phrase from one of the Holy Week narratives as its title and then focused attention upon the account of Jesus' last days from which that text was drawn. Implications for contemporary life were shaped by this exposition. These sermons, therefore, could be classified as textual with, perhaps, expository overtones. My hope is that preachers now and in time to come will connect what they say to the Bible more directly and fully than we did half a century ago.

Despite our limited use of the Bible, especially in the Advent series, these sermons were authentic proclamations in the context of Christian worship. Their power was rooted in their connection to the existential feeling of the moment. Listeners could recognize their everyday experiences—especially their deepening anxieties—in these sermons. Power also came from the clarity with which the sermons articulated the "chastened liberal evangelicalism," which preachers and congregants shared. Osborn used this phrase in a book (published in 1958) to describe the prevailing form of American Christianity. It is, he wrote, "essentially the traditional faith of the Christian church, incorporating certain liberal concepts and certain neo-orthodox correctives."[2] Although we undoubtedly differed in the details, we four preachers were united in the general pattern of theological understanding that we had learned in mainstream Protestant seminaries. Furthermore, the people who filled the pews week after week came to churches like University Christian because in these faith communities they found it possible to connect with the God whom Jesus embodied and at the same time live harmoniously within the intellectual world shaped by the physical and social sciences so highly regarded in modern American universities.

A striking characteristic of these sermons is the virtual absence of storytelling and anecdotal material. For their emotional connection with hearers, the preachers depended upon the sheer force of the ideas, their use of current conditions, such as communes in Seattle, and the personal impact of the preachers upon

---

2. Osborn, *The Spirit of American Christianity*, 169.

their hearers. While fulfilling one purpose of preaching, which is to declare that the gospel offers deliverance from the challenges of life, the sermons gave little attention to another basic feature of preaching, which is to offer what Hans van der Geest calls "evidential experience." In his book based on many interviews of people seeking therapy in a pastoral care center, he insists that what persuades hearers is not the theological power or correctness of the sermon but the living relationship of people, including the preacher, that has persuasive power.[3] People want to find ways to overcome the challenges that they are facing. They seek deliverance and are ready to believe the good news of the gospel that pastors offer them. Even so, they hesitate. Is it really true? Dare I believe and move forward in the way that is being proposed? The persuasive answers to these questions, van der Geest writes, are examples of changed lives. People seeking new life need to know that the ideas being proposed have worked for the preacher and for other people like themselves who now are living in strong and confident ways.

Preachers sometimes use anecdotal material to gain or establish a personal connection with the congregation or to maintain the listeners' attention; sometimes to lighten up a section of heavy prose; maybe even because they can't think of anything else to say. These uses are peripheral to the basic content of sermons. For van der Geest, however, personal examples have one purpose only, and it is crucial to the effectiveness of preaching: to show that the message for life that a sermon presents can be trusted and to encourage people to let their lives be reshaped accordingly.

Although our quartette of Seattle preachers seemed more accustomed to discussing ideas than to telling stories, evidential experience would not have been alien to our sermons and it is likely that the sermons would have been more effective had we included stories of the kind that van der Geest recommends. In the fifth Lenten sermon, "Do Not Weep for Me," Thomas included a set of examples from current life. Although they were but brief allusions, they brought to mind a long list of people who in the tragic world right then represented the faith that the preacher had been

---

3. van der Geest, *Presence in the Pulpit*, 120–21.

describing. And then, intellectual that he was, he drove the message home with a quotation from philosopher Alfred North Whitehead. There is "an element in our constitution that sees the tragedy as 'a living agent persuading the world to aim at fitness beyond the faded level of surrounding fact. Each tragedy is the disclosure of an ideal; what might have been and was not. What can be. The tragedy is not in vain.'"

Was this experiment in preaching successful? That is, should preachers and other church leaders of our time follow the example provided by the Seattle preachers half a century ago and develop their own series of sermons on the two foundational episodes in the emergence of the Christian faith? In one word, my answer is "yes." The inspiring story of the baby born in a manger who became the Suffering Servant bringing new life to a world in travail is the one story that Christians need to know and share with all the world. The Seattle sermons provide one model for how such sermons could be prepared and proclaimed. The collegial process of sermon preparation, that combines serious conversation, composition, and evaluation of sermons as they are being developed and delivered, can be theologically and spiritually invigorating to the preachers and congregants. Developing sermons like these is worth doing again from time to time.

Having a collegium of ordained preachers, however, is not a necessary factor. In addition to one or more clergy, other Christians with well-formed faith and communicative skills could be part of the team. The title of the Advent series is a better model than the title of the Lenten series because it announces the full scope of the series, whereas the Lenten title does not indicate that the tragic vision leads to the Easter hope. The sermonic form of the Lenten series, however, is preferable to that of the Advent series because the sermons are more fully grounded in the biblical narratives. Every sermon needs to include a clear description of the challenge that people face in life and a strong declaration of how the Christian faith helps us resolve that challenge.

Early in their conversations, the preachers should identify what they believe to be the central idea or ideas of the faith that they and congregants share. They should bring out clearly the biblical foundations of the sermons and ideas that are being presented in the sermons. They also need to confirm their sermons with evidential experience in order to lead their congregants into deeper faith.

I don't remember that we talked about publishing our "Dialogues on the Incarnation" either as weekly leaflets or as a book containing all of them. Since a full typescript was prepared for each Sunday, it would have been possible to move quickly to create a published version. Every-Sunday worshipers had to depend upon memory to follow the full thrust of what was being proclaimed. People who missed a Sunday had little sense of what was proclaimed in the sermon they missed. Today, of course, many churches post sermons online where they can be read or listened to. Even so, there is value in editing series of sermons such as these into pamphlets or books for distribution in the church, for use in the congregation's program of religious education, and perhaps for formal publication.

Two generations after these "Dialogues on the Incarnation" were preached, the names and places have changed, but we still are living in a time that needs sermons that can offer hope to distraught people. Susanne Langer's words that seemed exactly right in 1967–68 continue to ring true: "we feel ourselves swept along in a violent passage, from a world we cannot salvage to one we cannot see; and most people are afraid." What better time could there be than this to share the good news that Jesus, the Babe born in Bethlehem and the one whom God raised from the dead on Easter Day, is indeed "the way, the truth, and the life" (John 14:6)!

The Enduring Legacy

Robert Thomas began his ministry at University Christian Church on September 1, 1961, following the fourteen-year pastorate of John Paul Pack. During those post-World War II years, churches across the country were enjoying a period of remarkable growth. Some 3,030 persons had been received into membership during Pack's ministry, and the church's educational program and range of pastoral services had been enriched. The church's primary worship space had been renovated and a new chapel and youth activities facility constructed. The congregation had sponsored and funded a five-year "Abundant Life Program" for people in India, primarily in the fields of literacy and literature, health, and agriculture. As Thomas began his ministry, this sense of energy continued. The church purchased two hundred feet of property across from the church buildings on 15th Avenue Northeast to develop for parking. Income from houses on the property helped make payments until the church was ready to prepare the site for parking.[1]

In the brief history of the congregation that Thomas wrote in 1965, he noted that "total active membership of the church had declined from the high marks of the 1950s, with 1,599 members listed for 1964. The high level of giving during the period of renovation and construction had not been maintained, but the church's finances were strong. Attendance at church school and worship "had leveled off." Even so, he concluded his history with a strong

---

1. Thomas, *A Sketch of the History of University Christian Church.*

statement: "University Christian Church is uniquely situated in its history, physical facilities, and the theological freedom to receive God's gifts of unity and joy, and to make its witness relevant and strong." Thomas seemed unable—or perhaps unwilling—to understand why attendance and membership were declining. He was convinced that the seriousness of the gospel message he was proclaiming and the constructive character of all the church was doing should bring people into its life. Instead, as he told me one day, "they are leaving in droves."

He continued to devote much of his pastoral energy to helping the congregation participate in pioneering ministries in its part of the city, and these were continued by pastors who followed him as leaders of the congregation. During the 1970s and 80s, University Christian sponsored Latchkey, an afterschool program for local children. Changing neighborhood demographics, the closure of nearby University Heights School, and the emergence of similar programs in the area ended the latchkey program, but in time a cooperative daycare took over the same space at University Christian Church. In that same period of time, the church also provided a day program for seniors. For many decades, the congregation offered use of the building at no charge or well below market rates to twelve-step and other groups, and it dedicated space to a number of nonprofit organizations, including in recent decades the University District Food Bank, Books to Prisoners, the Seattle Human Services Coalition, and Northwest Health Law Advocates.

University Christian Church was also an active player in several important ecumenical ministries. In the 1990s, the U District congregations banded together to offer a youth shelter that rotated among church buildings in the District, following the murder of a teenage girl sleeping on the streets. Ultimately, that program was consolidated into the Roots Shelter for young adults at University Methodist Temple. The churches also hosted the Teen Feed program through that period.

University Christian was the first U District congregation to host Nickelsville, a homeless tent encampment that emerged in 2008 in response to sweeps of informal homeless camps sanctioned by Seattle's mayor at that time, Greg Nickels, and which moved every few months. Despite the City administration's threats to impose heavy fines on the congregation, Nickelsville spent two months on the UCC parking lot.

When these dialogue sermons were preached, it is unlikely that the four preachers or anyone else in the congregation was remembering an editorial that Harold E. Fey, one of the most prominent voices in American Protestantism, had published in the *Christian Century* magazine in 1958, stating that 1957 was the year that the post-World War II return to religion passed crest. After a decade of unprecedented growth, church attendance across the country was slipping, in some congregations as protests of stances toward public affairs that pastors were taking. Often, however, as an Indianapolis pastor told one of my classes at the seminary, people weren't mad; they simply were slipping away one by one. As later studies of religion and public life across the country have documented, this process was especially evident in the Pacific Northwest, which came to be identified as "The None Zone." In the introduction to a book on religion in this region of the country, Patricia O'Connell Killen writes that the "defining feature of religion in the Pacific Northwest is that most of the population is 'unchurched.' Fewer people in Oregon, Washington, and Alaska affiliate with a religious institution than in any other region of the United States."[2]

Even if all else had remained unchanged, the slipping away from religious affiliation would have been more pronounced in a university community than in most other urban and residential settings. In Seattle, however, additional factors accelerated that tendency. One was the steady growth of the University of Washington on its 703-acre main campus in Seattle. In 1970, the university enrolled some 32,000 students, but by 2019 the campus facilities had expanded significantly and enrollment had increased by more than ten thousand. Compounding the pressure was the construction during the late 1950s and early 1960s of Interstate-5 through Seattle's long, narrow tract of land tightly bound by Puget Sound on the west and Lake Washington on the east. The section of this freeway that runs along Fifth Avenue Northeast a few blocks west of

---

2. Killen and Silk, *Religion and Public Life in the Pacific Northwest*, 9.

the university destroyed a significant number of homes and created a barrier dividing this part of the city into two isolated neighborhoods. This double squeeze, resulting in enlarged student population and diminished residential housing, contributed to dramatic increases in housing costs and decreased residential population. A barometer of these changes was University Heights School only two blocks from University Christian Church. It opened in 1903 and in 1920 reached its peak enrollment of over nine hundred students. In 1988, the school enrolled 138 in its regular K-5 program and 213 in its K-6 alternative elementary school No. 2. In 1989, despite community opposition to the action, the district closed University Heights School. The architecturally significant building remains as the University Heights Center and is headquarters for various community-oriented organizations and service programs.

Throughout this period of community and congregational change, University Christian Church was ably led by a continuing line of competent, committed pastors and lay leaders. It maintained educational and service opportunities for constituents. Sunday after Sunday, worship was celebrated with strong music, articulate preaching, and reverent administrations of Holy Communion. Even so, there was a gradual but continuing diminishing of participation by its members and a corresponding thinning out of new people. Other churches along Fifteenth Avenue Northeast and nearby streets dealt with similar challenges, but University Christian was affected more seriously than some of the others. In time, it was necessary to rearrange front pews in its thousand-seat church so that worshipers, sometimes fewer than fifty persons, could sit close to one another and feel their participation in the worshiping community.

In December 2015, University Christian Churched reached the culmination of a twenty-year dream to provide affordable housing in the university district. With funding provided by the Seattle Office of Housing and other agencies, and in cooperation with a not-for-profit agency in the city, the church transformed its parking lot into Arbora Court, a multi-story, 133-unit apartment building for families with incomes ranging from 0 to 60 percent of the area median income (and with parking that would be available for the church's use). The total cost of the project was nearly $40,000,000.

Soon after this project was completed, however, leaders of the congregation, came to a long-postponed conclusion that University Christian Church could no longer be sustained in its historic location and in direct continuity with the congregation that had existed since 1890. The Service of Celebration that concluded the history of this congregation in Seattle's University district took place on July 21, 2018. Two of the quartette of dialogue preachers, Gene Kidder and Tom McCormick, who had continued as members of this church through this half century, were among the leaders of the service. The large sum of money realized from the sale of University Christian Church's site, nearly three-quarters of an acre, was used to create a fund that is administered by a board of directors for the purpose of supporting educational institutions, ecclesial organizations, and community programs that have been at the center of University Christian Church's life and ministry. One legacy that this historic church leaves to the city of Seattle where it has ministered since 1890 is embodied in Arbora Court and the University Christian Church Foundation, which are strong, institutional manifestations of the congregation's long-time commitments that will ensure that these values will long continue.

A second legacy also continues, and here I turn to a group of essays on Protestant liberalism by Berkeley historian David A. Hollinger.[3] He emphasizes that until about 1960 virtually everyone in places of leadership, in government, business, education, and other aspects of American life, was identified with one of the ecumenical Protestant churches. Since then, that dominance has shifted significantly. Jews and Catholics are much more prominent than they once were. Equally important is the rise of evangelical Protestantism. Hollinger emphasizes two reasons for this shift in the balance of power among the churches. The more important is that the leaders of ecumenical churches embraced and promulgated within their constituencies important changes in basic cultural and social

---

3. Hollinger, *After Cloven Tongues of Fire*. Ecumenical Protestant churches is the term Hollinger uses in reference to progressive or mainline Protestant churches.

principles. These churches "were caught in the ferocious cross-fire of national controversies over all the classic issues of the period, especially civil rights, Vietnam, empire, feminism, abortion, and sexual orientation." Their memberships declined, and conservative, evangelical churches, which upheld earlier understandings of these issues, gained dramatically. Hollinger gives his own twist to one of the demographic trends of the period. The birthrate among liberal Protestants declined, in large part, because their members espoused and practiced some of these new values, whereas the birthrate among conservative Protestants stayed high because they rejected those same values. He notes that the conservative churches were more effective than the liberal in retaining their youth.

One of Hollinger's conclusions is that "the United States of today, even with the prominence of politically conservative evangelical Protestants, looks much more like the country ecumenical leaders of the 1960s hoped it would become than the one their evangelical rivals sought to create." Sociologist N. J. Demerath III, Hollinger continues, "has put this point hyperbolically: the ecumenical Protestants scored a 'cultural victory' while experiencing 'organizational defeat.'"[4]

Seattle is one of the nation's liberal, pace-setting cities. Following Hollinger's lead, I think it can be said that the left-leaning culture of this progressive city is, in part, a legacy of the U District's ecumenical Protestant churches, including University Christian Church and its witness from 1890 through 2018. Although this congregation no longer opens its doors to people seeking direction, hope, and courage, its theological and cultural legacy continues. And this legacy, especially if it inspires new sermons at a time when "all creation groans in travail, waiting for its redemption," can inspire us to look forward, waiting and working for the time when "creation will be set free from its bondage" (adapted from Rom 8:19–21).

---

4. Hollinger, *After Cloven Tongues of Fire*, 14; see also 46–47.

Advent Dialogues:
Born to Set the People Free

Advent 1: Bound

Robert A. Thomas

The theme, "Born to Set the People Free," is a statement of the meaning of the incarnation found in "Come, Thou Long Expected Jesus," an Advent hymn composed by Charles Wesley in 1744 as an expression of the fulfillment of Israel's messianic expectation. Wesley was an Anglican who experienced such a sense of the presence and call of God in a Moravian meeting house in London in 1738 that his life was changed and his purposes redirected so that—together with his brother, John, who underwent a similar conversion—they were responsible for the birth of the Methodist Church. Charles became a prolific hymn writer, and the singing of hymns a most important means of arousing the lethargic, encouraging the faithful, and educating the ignorant. He wrote 6,500 hymns on every conceivable phase of Christian experience and Methodist theology and published a total of fifty-six collections of hymns in small tracts and full-scale books! The hymns are "intense, purposeful, and introspective," as one author has said, yet at the same time socially concerned. They are humble, on the one hand, but militant, on the other; for Wesley was certain that "religion, salvation, character, and the will to save others were the most important things in the world."[1]

---

1. Blake, *The Gospel in Hymns*, 82–85.

Advent Dialogues: Born to Set the People Free

>Come, thou long-expected Jesus,
>Born to set thy people free;
>From our fears and sins release us,
>Let us find our rest in thee.
>
>Israel's Strength and Consolation,
>Hope of all the saints thou art;
>Dear Desire of every nation,
>Joy of every longing heart.
>
>Born, thy people to deliver,
>Born a child, and yet a King,
>Born to reign in us forever,
>Now thy gracious Kingdom bring.
>
>By thine own eternal Spirit,
>Rule in all our hearts alone;
>By thine all-sufficient merit,
>Raise us to thy glorious throne.

By the time Christmas comes, this hymn and its music ought to have particularly significant meaning for us all.

The word "we" used in reference to choosing the theme and finding the hymn was not editorial. Four of us are engaged in an experiment in preaching this Advent season, seeking to clarify the ways in which people of our time see themselves in relation to the traditions of the faith, the characteristic factors in our culture, and the current meaning of the incarnation. Let it be clear at the outset that we have no intention of setting up some kind of phony "conversation" here in the pulpit. We will not be actors playing parts. We will be what we are ordained to be: ministers proclaiming the gospel. What we will preach is being carefully prepared, and what we finally declare will be the product (in some ways, at least) of all our minds in dialogue. It is, frankly, an experiment, so far as I know, not performed before. But it is an exciting and stimulating enterprise for us, and we hope it will be for all of you, too.

My task in this sermon is twofold: first, to introduce the series, and to enlist your thoughtful participation; and, second, to attempt to describe the ways in which the subject is relevant to the world of

Advent 1: Bound

our time. The general title, "Born to Set the People Free," suggests that we believe that people in the twentieth century, as in the first, are chained, confined, imprisoned, and enslaved; that modern men and women are bound, too. The title implies that we are committed to the faith that Christ was and is a "deliverer" and that twentieth-century people need to be delivered as desperately as first-century people.

The pop song, "Born Free," originally referred to an animal in a movie, and that was, perhaps, appropriate. It may be that Elsa the Lion was born "As free as the wind blows . . . As free as the grass grows . . . Born free to follow your heart," as the song declares. But it is being sung by folk singers and heard by audiences as if it related to humans, and that is sheer nonsense.

No one is born free. All freedom is either given or achieved. We are born into a particular family, community, region, nation, culture, religion, and race. If you're born black in Alabama you're not born free. If you were born a Jew in Nazi Germany you were not born free. If you're born in an outcast village in the Central Provinces in India you're not born free. Or if you're born an American Indian on the Yakama Reservation you're not born free. But neither are you born free if you're the child of a middle-class, reasonably happy, white, Anglo-Saxon, Protestant family in Seattle or the Middle West or anywhere else.

Think how people in our time are bound. There are, in the first place, internal mechanisms of control about which we have come to know a good deal in the past generation or so. All of us are creatures of habit, attitudes, and belief systems we have gradually absorbed. Not many of us have chosen the basic direction of life. They have been given us by the family and culture of our birth. Some of us in the process of education, experience, travel, and reflection have managed to examine some of what we have absorbed, and now and then choices are made that mark a turned direction. But in terms of the whole human race in our time such choices are rare. And even in terms of the congregation present this morning (or any other like it across the land) such changes of direction, habits, attitudes, and belief systems are most unusual.

We are bound, too, by emotional conflicts, physical drives, and motivations out of consciousness but nonetheless real. An untold amount of unhappiness and crime and personal strife occur for reasons that are never known to the people involved. The basic conflicts are buried and the conscious mind rationalizes what happens, giving an acceptable reason for action which is not the real reason at all. None of us entirely escapes; all of us are bound by what is outside our conscious minds but controls to some degree the way we act.

Among these internal mechanisms of control must be counted, too, the ego-protecting "will-to-live" and "will-to-power." They are part of our makeup as human beings, necessary to our survival in the evolutionary process. But in terms of human need in the modern world they are chains and shackles. The fear of death and the fear of dependence (loss of power) are deep-seated in the modern world; indeed, perhaps even more so than in the first century. And what about the fear of failure that is so pervasive and that is such a powerful obstacle to growth? Children are great risk-takers, but they quickly learn the meaning of failure and little by little quit taking the risks, progressively narrowing the personality and stifling exploration and experimentation.

Some of us are bound because we have never been loved. Our parents *used* us for their purposes, *managed* us for their satisfactions, *found meanings* for their own lives only in ours. They never loved us for ourselves. There are more persons in our society like that than any of us want to admit, and never having been loved they find it difficult or impossible to love. They are dwarfed emotionally; their humanity severely limited or perhaps stifled altogether. And that means they are bound.

I have only a moment or two to speak of some of the emotional forces and factors in our environment that contribute to the condition described by the word "bound." John Gardner, Secretary of Health, Education, and Welfare, writes in his book *Self-Renewal* of the web of fixed relationships, the weight of tradition, vested interests, and modern, large scale organizations (among other factors) as contributing to the prevention of renewal. What he really is saying is that persons and businesses and institutions (including government) may be bound by these characteristic elements in the life of our time.

The routines of life, the regular going and coming of work and family and even pleasure, stifle creativity, thwart our humanity. We lose the capacity to see; the comfortable web imprisons us so that we "don't know that we've been imprisoned until after we've broken out."[2] Who is there who hasn't had something of that experience when the company transferred the head of the family, or when sudden and serious illness meant changing jobs or location, and perhaps everything else.

Tradition weighs heavy upon us, particularly so in religious life and institutions. Tradition is that body of customs, standards, rules, and regulations (written or unwritten), the underbrush of precedent which is part of all our life. It can have an oppressive effect on creativity. Too much dependence on it, reverence for it, means that we are less flexible, less innovative, less willing to look freshly at each day's experience. Great concern with tradition means an inordinate emphasis on the appropriateness of behavior, and as Mr. Gardner says, it can result in the channeling of all our energy into "tiny rivulets of conformity."[3] That does not mean all tradition is bad, any more than that webs of relationship are all bad. But how often have you heard the phrase, "bound by tradition?"

One needs only to hear the words "vested interests" to be reminded how we are bound by our possessions and love of possessions. Accumulations weight one down and the status quo looks better the more the possessions pile up. William James said, "Lives based on having are less free than lives based either on doing or on being."[4] Think how our institutions are bound by vested interests. "The buildings grow bigger and the spirit thins out." One wonders how the church will ever be a servant church, how the people of God will ever become a servant people, when there is as much concern for buildings and special tax privileges and property rights as

---

2. Gardner, *Self-Renewal*, 9.

3. Gardner, *Self-Renewal*, 48.

4. Gardner, *Self-Renewal*, 51, citing James, *Varieties of Religious Experience*, 313.

there is among us today. Who would deny that we are bound by our possessions?

Or that we are bound by the large-scale organizations of modern life? Technology demands larger and larger groupings, more and more impersonal connections. Corporations are so large and varied in operation they defy the imagination. The development of atomic power, the completion of an electric power grid over the whole country, the exploration of space—all of them are examples of large-scale organization natural to modern society. And it is nearly inevitable in such a society that there is a constant search for common denominators and ways of standardization; that there is preoccupation with method, techniques, and procedures; that there is a homogenization of culture. If the sheer size of organizations developed by modern technology is not to destroy us, those who manage the processes must be firmly committed to the preservation and extension of aesthetic, spiritual, and social values. And I have grave doubt that that is now the case.

We could go on. Modern people are bound by ignorance, by poverty, by the conventions and superficialities of life, and by too much specialization. You can add to the list. What has the incarnation to do with all this? Does Christ come yet to set the people free? That is our faith; that in the midst of the life of the world—this world of business and organization and specialization and conformities and institutions and fear of death and unconscious powers and motivations—Christ comes. He brings liberty to the captives and the opening of the prison to those who are bound.

Advent 2: Doing Your Own Thing

Thomas R. McCormick and Robert A. Thomas

Thomas: A great many persons in our time feel themselves bound. Caught in a web of relationships from which they cannot escape, conditioned by internal mechanisms out of their control, pressured by external forces in the environment, trapped by the heavy weight of traditions and vested interests, some desperately seek a way out. While most members of the society conform to the standards of value, patterns of culture, and ways of life of the majority, some actively promote other systems of value, forms of thought, and styles of life.

In a university community, such as this, we are more aware than most, perhaps, of such movements of protest and reform. On the university campus itself, and all around us in the District, are the visible evidences of non-conformity. For the most part, these people have had no experience of the one who was "born to set the people free." They may have had some limited church connection, but if so, it has seemed to them more imprisoning than liberating, so that many of them are in active revolt against institutional religion and some of them believe the church to be the most powerful of all the protectors of the status quo and the false values of the culture, an enemy of personal freedom and social reform.

We cannot really know the world in which we live, nor project relevant ways of life and work for the church, nor become a servant people of God, apart from the serious effort to listen to those who are not only critics of "the establishment," but honestly seek to assert their freedom and humanity over against the de-humanizing forces and confining powers present and active in our world. In recent years the hippie movement has attracted nationwide attention. Articles describing this subculture have appeared in newspapers and slick journals, and here in our District no one can overlook the existence and importance of a movement that attracts so many adherents and influences so many others one way or another.

McCormick: In an era which seems to demand a great deal of organization of one's time and life, and encourages conformity rather than individuality, the hippie is one who might best be characterized as the person who insists that the important thing is to "hang loose" from all of this, and just "do your own thing." The original hippies were young people who believed in a gentle philosophy of nonviolence, love, and freedom from society's standards, with a heavy emphasis on the individualistic style of living. Hippies set themselves apart from "straight" society, and for the most part are against the establishment. They are critics of the war in Vietnam, nuclear weapons, computers, and automation (although they are grateful for the technology which made production of LSD-25 possible). Most "straights" cannot understand how hippies can be happy in their old clothes, long hair, bare feet, and beads. Nor do they understand the apparent joy of hippies at a "Happening" or "Be In," when hundreds of young people come to dance, sing, paint flowers on faces and hands, and talk beside the burning incense sticks. One of the big differences between the hip and straight community is the hippie's failure to take seriously the ideals, goals, and standards of the majority. In reaction, a hippie ends up giving a greater degree of seriousness to the little things—the picnics, a song, a piece of carved wood, an unusual article of clothing, or a friend's new poem.

Advent 2: Doing Your Own Thing

The focus is on the individual and the importance of the thing he or she chooses to do.

Another factor which is difficult for many people to understand is the apparent disregard for the law which is evidenced by many in the hippie community, specifically in reference to draft resistance and the possession and use of illegal drugs. This is an extension of the highly individualistic style of life which encourages one to disregard a law which seems to stifle personal pleasure or conflict with a person's basic orientation to life.

There is a transient nature to the hippie scene, a coming and going. Most hippies range from the teens to the thirties and at the upper end there is a procession of those who have "done their thing," who drop out of hippiedom and re-enter society. Often the new candidates for the barbershop are those who have simply grown tired of being hungry and cold and frustrated both by lack of funds and meaningful employment. Often, too, when marriage and the prospect of the birth of children occur, a new dimension of interdependence and responsibility enters the picture.

In San Francisco during the summer of 1967, the Hippie Movement was buried. There was a coffin, a wake, and a period of mourning. Tourists, violence, and the mass media have ruined their scene. But the funeral seems to have been a little premature, for the hippie is still quite visibly evident, and "doing your own thing" has not ceased to be important. One change in the hippie scene is the movement on the part of many toward the formation of small groups of six to twelve who institute a pattern of communal living. It is generally agreed that the groups gathered on "The Ave" or "42nd St." are for the most part the teenagers, the "teeny-boppers," the loners, and the newcomers. This seems to be the "induction center" for new hippies; the older, the wiser, and the more mature are found elsewhere.

Thomas: It is perfectly evident to any observer that many different kinds of persons are involved in the hippie movement. And it has become increasingly clear that they are attracted to it for a variety of reasons. One hears stories of youngsters fifteen or so running away from home and finding refuge among the hippies in San Francisco or here in Seattle. And one hears of bizarre forms of group meditation or "worship" and the general practice of the use of drugs. And one talks to persons who consider themselves part of "the scene" and yet are greatly different in terms of emotional need and maturity. All these variations and differences force one to try to discover what the real factors are that underlie this mood or attract persons to this movement.

McCormick: How and why did the hippies come into being? The answer is not simple, for a number of factors are involved. In the first place, many more families than formerly know the meaning of the phrase "absentee father." The pressures of the culture keep them from assuming a strong leadership role in family life, and the children feel the deprivation. A recent song, "Child of Clay," is a protest against unloving parents. One of the lines reads: "and the father, thinking work comes first, did not take time to quench the thirst." In many cases there has been a lack of identification of sons with their fathers and a failure of some to appropriate the strength of their own manhood.

Some young people join the hippie movement as a form of adolescent rebellion. There is probably no more potent a threat to parents than the idea of their son or daughter running with the hippies or smoking pot. And this becomes the very way a significant number of adolescents act out their desire for emancipation and freedom from parental control.

One of the aspects of life in the hippie scene is the use of drugs. Marijuana has been heralded by the hippie community as a real asset to mankind, and they have pretty largely blown the earlier mythology that marijuana should be classified with the harder and addictive drugs such as heroin. There any many evangelists for the drug cult. We have all heard of the hallucinatory aspects of LSD and others that are currently used. The continuing use of drugs to produce a "high" feeling of euphoria is a highly individualistic act. One's feeling of well-being is not really grounded in reality, nor is it related to one's involvement with other people; it is, rather, a chemically produced sensation which soon disappears. Contrary to popular notion in the hippie world that drugs are mind-expanding and consciousness-enlarging, it is more precise to say that the use of drugs often narrows the range of a person's relationships, turns him inward on himself, and relies on introspection to produce a sense of meaning that has not been found in the real world. Some people find support for their non-success in this kind of activity.

On the other hand, there are those within the hippie community who are appreciative of the good in our culture, but who are forthrightly critical of what seems to them de-humanizing and destructive. Their efforts are not intended to be hostile, but positive and creative. They seek to reform bad attitudes and practice and release us from the impersonal powers of our environment and culture in which we are bound. We may feel the means they choose are not always the most cogent and powerful, but we should give attention to their word. One may find these more mature persons grouped together in a house somewhere trying to maintain a certain style of life to which they are committed, and to preserve it within their little subgroup. There is a sense in which their way of life is reminiscent of the monastic style of earlier times, in which a certain purity of life and belief was preserved by those who drew apart from the world to avoid its perversions. Some hippies are sensitive and reflective persons who suffer concerning the problems of our society, but who feel powerless and impotent to change the great power complexes which so affect the destiny of us all. Nevertheless, they protest, often in the only means which seem an option, by the refusal to buy the establishment, and by their own independent stand as persons for the qualities of life in which they believe.

Thomas: Reaction to the presence of the hippie crowd in our midst (on the Avenue, or the campus, or perhaps even in the sanctuary and halls of the church) varies from good-natured toleration to determined efforts to wipe them out; from genuine interest and concern to the curiosity of the gawking tourist. Some people want to know, "Why bother? There aren't many of them, really. Why such a fuss about a tiny minority of our youth?"

Lane Smith, religion editor for the *Seattle Times*, listened in on one of the planning sessions for this sermon. Besides contributing his own knowledge and interest, he made the interesting observation that every time the newspaper prints a story about the hippies, no matter what its content, they get a flood of calls and letters from people wanting to know, "Who cares? Why do you write about these people?" But the five of us agreed that the stories are read: There is a very great deal of interest in what is a tiny minority among our youth.

McCormick: It is evident that some people see the hippies as a very serious threat to our traditional social structure, a feeling shared by Assemblyman John Burton of the Haight-Asbury District in San Francisco. Some cannot tolerate their nonconformity to social customs and dress. Others live in fear of their disrespect for laws and authority, in spite of the gentle and nonviolent philosophy to which most hippies adhere. Parents see them as a potential threat to their children, with a kind of "Pied Piper fantasy" about their power of attraction. Police see them as constant law violators who are hard to catch and difficult to prosecute. The real "straight" sees them as dropouts from society, and some groups act out their hostility toward hippies in open and aggressive persecution.

On the other hand, there seems to be evidence that there may be a subconscious desire on the part of many people to join the hippies. There is a certain childlike quality which may invite us to take a vacation from the responsibilities with which we are beset. One professor at the University of Washington has described the hippie movement as a return to childhood, with pre-occupation with play and flowers and clothes. All of us live with impulses to avoid responsibility, to break the tight-knit schedule of our day with some aesthetic delight, but usually we are held in check by our sense of duty, by our ability to organize out the distracting influences, or by our commitment to some larger purpose. Nevertheless, the impulse is often there. Perhaps that is why some are tolerant of the hippies, and others smile faintly and discreetly at their approach, and still others slip off to Haight-Asbury or some other out-of-town community for a weekend of hanging loose and "doing your own thing."

Thomas: Once again, we have to ask what does the incarnation have to do with all of this? We have proclaimed our faith that in the midst of the life of the world—this world of business and organization and specialization and conformities and institutions and fear of death and unconscious powers and motivations—Christ comes to set the people free; that he brings liberty to the captives and the opening of the prison to those who are bound. Is there any connection between freedom in Christ and the freedom of the hippie? Or, if there is no connection, what are the differences?

McCormick: There is certainly a kind of freedom in the hippie style. There is little sense of obligation or responsibility to anyone. There is freedom from schedule, in many cases a freedom from work, a freedom to do as you choose up to a point. There is a freedom from conforming to traditional moral standards. There is a freedom from obeying the law, unless you are arrested, without feeling guilty. But is this the kind of freedom we want, and which is really helpful to mankind? Over one hundred years ago Soren Kierkegaard made a comparison of the aesthetic man and the ethical man which is helpful at this point. The aesthetic man is one who is committed to the seeking and fulfillment of his own pleasure. He is basically a hedonist. His only commitment is to the development of his own happiness, and his greatest enemies are changes in mood which might alone spoil an otherwise perfect occasion. His pleasure is the only thing he can take seriously, and even that is not really a serious matter. On the contrary, an ethical man takes his ethical responsibility seriously. He allows for it to impinge upon his aesthetic pleasure, for it is a more serious commitment, and must take first priority, even though he cannot guarantee that his efforts will be successful.

A psychiatrist in this community spoke recently of another factor in our human situation when he said: "Every person needs a meaningful employment of his particular talents, and the opportunity to give and receive intimacy." Too frequently, both of these factors are missing in the hippie community, because there is no investment of its members in a serious task and insufficient basis of trust from which such intimacy may spring.

Too often, the "love" idea of the hippies, which is meant to go beyond and transcend a shallow cultural image of romanticism, is only a cultural reflection or affectation which lacks real commitment. Two ideas which do not fit nicely together at all, but are basically opposed to each other, are the concept of love in the radical sense in which it was used in the gospel, and the easy conscience about "doing your own thing" with a good feeling toward other people. The idea of love in the gospel took the form of a strong commitment to the other, a responsible limitation of one's selfish desires in order to act on that priority, and a willingness at times even to suffer for the sake of the other. The result is a community of persons which is highly interdependent, life not bounded and circumscribed by laws and regulations, but truly free because of a covenant and promise sealed by the gift of God in Christ.

Thomas: What we have to say is that many of the goals and ideas of the people who think of themselves as hippies are very important, as are some of their criticisms of the phony manners and conventions of the "straight" world. But they are only kidding themselves if they think they have discovered any significant freedom in "doing your own thing." The only freedom worthy of the name is freedom within structures, freedom that comes

Advent 2: Doing Your Own Thing

in loyalty and devotion to what is beyond the self. It is the freedom of the "man in Christ," the freedom of one who has discovered who he is and what his life is because he has confronted God in the "man for others." It is the freedom of life in the covenant community established by response to the gift of God in Christ.

Dag Hammarskjöld, the secretary-general of the United Nations whose tragic death in 1961 shocked the world, left behind the manuscript of a book. Many of us have read its pages with surprise. We had admired the public man; we had not really known the depth of his commitment to the Way of the Cross. Hammarskjöld himself described the manuscript as a "sort of white book concerning my negotiations with myself and with God." Toward the end is this entry on Whitsunday, 1961:

> I don't know who—or what—put the question. I don't know when it was put. I don't even remember answering. But at some moment I did answer Yes to Someone—or Something—and from that hour I was certain that existence is meaningful and that, therefore, my life, in self-surrender, had a goal. From that moment I have known what it means "not to look back," and "to take no thought for the morrow."[1]

That is the freedom that comes, not in isolation, not in dropping out, not in disconnection from tradition, not in irresponsibly "doing your own thing," but only through getting your history straight, and in commitment, response, and self-surrender to the God who makes himself know in Jesus Christ—"the man for others" who was "born to set the people free."

---

1. Hammarskjöld, *Markings*, 205.

Advent 3: Getting Your History Straight

Eugene Kidder and Robert A. Thomas

Thomas: One of the members of the congregation responded to the first sermon in this series with the question, "Who wants to be free?" There was implied acknowledgment of the fact that people are bound, even in this modern world of instant communication and rapid transportation, but a recognition that many persons are satisfied in their bondage. And, of course, that is the case. Who can say what percentage of our population, or of our city, or of this congregation, truly want to be free (or, perhaps more to the point, what degree of bondage will they tolerate)? I don't know. But I do know that there is historical evidence that human beings seek freedom; that some persons are willing to die for it; that whole nations may bow to dictatorial control for periods of time, only sooner or later to rise against the autocracy that seeks to make them less than human. A strong case can be made for the presence of an inner demand in the being of people for the completion of their full humanity, only possible as they achieve freedom and become responsible persons.

From a theological point of view, this inner demand for fulfillment, for freedom, is the result of the way we are created by

God, and in the biblical story, the history of both individuals and a people reveals the way in which the purposes of God in the whole creation are being achieved. The desire for freedom, then, is part of our nature as human beings. And we are less than human when that desire is repressed, misunderstood, feared, or turned into destructive ways of being and acting.

Whatever the percentage is, many people who feel themselves bound, caught in a web of circumstances and relationships, do seek to become free. Some of them break loose from their home and community ties and join themselves to groups with dramatically different goals and practices (as some join the hippies) only to discover after a while that the energy and effort is misdirected and they are no more free than before.

The more usual reaction is to seek help from some friend or counselor. Statistics show that forty percent of the people in trouble go first to a minister. Pastors spend a lot of time with people who are unable to exercise their full humanity because they are in bondage.

Kidder: When people who are regularly engaged in the science and art of healing allow their mind's eye to scan the train of humanity which moves in and out of the consulting room, they first gaze in memory at walking death.

They come, orphans of affluence, crammed with earthly riches while sustaining the grim determination of inner poverty. The plain and the beautiful, the young and the old, sophisticated and simple, prestigious and disreputable—they all come, for soul-suffering is no respecter of persons. They come with their "hang-ups," as the current saying goes. It is no accidental term, for so many contemporary people have hung their own lives in effigy. Like T. S. Eliot's hollow, stuffed men, they have stored layer upon layer of their reality within their own being, until the motion of life is brought to a halt. The finely wrought parts of an orderly personality have been corroded.

They come as nomads in search of the selves they've never found, or lost, or left behind. Some are exiles, become alien to the creatures they one-time began to be, then surrendered to the enslavement of their own prison. I shall never forget the man who went skiing for the first time, felt strange, and found the stranger to be himself, whom he left in a snow bank during childhood. I will always recall the middle-aged woman who told me of whistling in her kitchen, and suddenly realizing she had not whistled like that since her teen years.

Like giant turtles they come, bearing on their backs the burdens of generations before them. They cringe inside the hulk of an outmoded identity, gasping for air they need so desperately before they can ever live as the choosing creatures God has given them to be. They knock on my door and the doors of psychiatrists, psychologists, and social workers, asking for the love they long for but cannot accept.

When they meet the reality of care and truth, they are skeptical, resistive, and afraid—most of all afraid! They are afraid the protective shells will be ripped off, leaving their raw, tender, weak spirits exposed to the elements. They are afraid that if they dare to enter the open air, some other needy soul will descend upon their morsel of life like a vulture and ravage their household. Most of all, they fear that they are destined to repeat the failures of the generations before them. The Scripture I have heard quoted most often in a counseling interview is usually given with a great sigh, "It is certainly true that 'the sins of the fathers are visited upon the children and the children's children to the third and fourth generation'" (Exod 34:7). People in trouble feel most deeply the worst that has happened to their parents and to them, and believe that it is all that *will* happen in the future. They deny themselves present joy for the sake of the future defeat they expect inevitably to follow. Whatever they say in words (and they may hold a great variety of philosophies or theologies) they are really determinists. They do not and cannot believe in freedom. Some of them believe they have already been condemned for the failures of others and have consigned themselves to a pit of despair. Dead on the inside, they savor the familiar misery and perform the dull routine. If by now it seems I must be referring to someone far away, be reminded that this may be your dear friend, or someone sitting next to you, or possibly yourself.

The condition itself is binding enough. The attempts to fight it often create a further bind. So, many people hide their history in a denial. But refusal to face their past increases its power over them. Some create a garden of Eden and shut the larger reality away. Some enslave themselves to work or family or pleasure or even to supreme well-doing. Underneath, they continue to relive the very patterns they want so much to escape.

Thomas: In the cynical view of history there is an endless repetition of circumstances and events with no significant change and no final purpose. Life and history are meaningless. Nietzsche has the animals say to Zarathustra:

> "Everything goeth, everything returneth; eternally rolleth the wheel of existence. Everything dieth, everything blossometh forth again; eternally runneth on the year of existence. Everything breaketh, everything is integrated anew; eternally buildeth itself the same house of existence. All things separate, all things again greet one another; eternally true to itself remaineth the ring of existence. Every moment beginneth existence, around every 'here' rolleth the ball 'there.' The middle is everywhere. Crooked is the path of eternity."[1]

But the biblical view of history is linear. Christians inherit from Jews the faith that the creation is of God and that it has meaning and purpose. It is moving toward an end, which in both Jewish and Christian terminology is the kingdom of God. And while there have been and are different understandings of the relation of the coming of the kingdom to human methods of reckoning time and the significance of human choice and action, still there is general agreement in the faith-community that there is direction in history, that it is moving toward the final purpose of God.

---

1. Nietzsche, *Thus Spoke Zarathustra*, 244.

But any depth perception of personal histories reveals the reality of cycles in our lives. We are the children of parents, the inheritors of patterns and attitudes, and again and again counselors see the humanity of persons stifled as they repeat the cycles of deprivation and fear and depression and marital discord over and over again.

What the biblical revelation makes plain is that those cycles must be broken so that the lives of individual men and women may be fulfilled—their histories become linear instead of circular.

Kidder: Hope comes to a sufferer when he gains the courage to face the worst of himself and his personal history. Demonic forces just cannot resist a challenge. When the promise of life steps forth, destructive influences are forced out of hiding, and that is the signal of their ultimate defeat. They cannot survive in the light. The first hard step is the very act of requesting help. The false notion that one can face and solve all of life's problems alone with nothing but his own resources has been dealt a serious blow.

When the same sufferer has tested his helper to the fullest extent and found that he is no fake; that he means and does what he says; and that he has received the person in order to truly help him, and not to satisfy some need of his own, another burst of hope springs up. From then forward it is only a matter of time. The powerful alliance into which the two people have entered increases in strength, until the death itself is placed beyond its power ever to capture the spirit of the person. Of course its threat will always remain, and even the most successfully treated person must remain forever vigilant to the possibility that evil may return at a more opportune time.

It is here that one of the profoundest realities of our Christian faith takes hold. History is the unfolding drama in which each successive event is the unique combination of people and influences to create an unrepeatable moment. God's recreative activity in the present allows the believer his chance to gather up the worst wreckage of his past, and its greatest riches, and create something new. How strikingly at times we see the gestures or mannerisms of a father or mother repeated in a son or daughter. But part of our attention is drawn by the very different style of expression in which the younger person reveals the similarity. The greater train of our historical faith declares that each generation has received an incorruptible inheritance, and that he may accept it and move beyond it to new territory for faithful service.

Joshua, knowing of the Exodus, received the promise at the River Jordan.

> This day I will begin to exalt you in the sight of all Israel, that they may know that, as I was with Moses, so I will be with you. And you shall command the priests who bear the Ark of the Covenant, "When you come to the waters of the Jordan, you shall stand in the Jordan" . . . and the people passed over opposite Jericho (Josh 3:7–8, 16c).

John the Baptist struggled with the sense that "after me comes one who is mightier than I, the thongs of whose sandals I am not worthy to stoop down and untie" (Mark 1:7); yet John himself would be called upon to baptize this Jesus who came into the world that men might know the complete freedom which John could only anticipate.

The counseling relationship is but a microcosm of the larger work of God in history. Together the counselor and counselee delicately and painfully lift each bit of spiritual tissue, scraping out the poison, discovering the life and health behind it, putting it back in place and waiting for recovery. As this is done, one begins to see the great gifts of his family. He discovers something fine which is not his own doing, yet he begins to do it as his own in a way that is unlike anything ever before seen upon the earth. He begins to feel a little lower than the angels, one who occupies a space in the universe which has never been occupied by any other creature. Like Joshua he can enter the troubled waters and stand. As the integration phase of his therapy occurs he redirects the vast energies which before he used to remain "captain of his soul," and which now can be channeled into personal fulfillment, a positive but human kind of life and service, the joy of being. Such an event in a person's life may be considered his participation in the death, burial, and resurrection of Jesus Christ.

Thomas: The use of those terms, so central to the establishment of the church and the meaning of the Christian faith, suggests (as does a great deal of what we have been saying) that we see this process of coming to full humanity, to freedom and dignity and responsibility, as taking place in a special way in the midst of the community of faith.

We are talking about a ministry the church establishes and supports out of its faith, and in connection with its fundamental mission to persons who are bound, and about the significance of the body of Christ itself in sustaining persons involved in this creative process. We see the context in which this liberating work with persons is carried on, and the faith stance and way of life of the counselor, as matters of crucial importance.

Kidder: All ministers, and in a particular way, the pastoral counselor, engage in processes of redemption like those we have described. We do this work as we can. We also support and encourage it through community agencies or those who labor in private consulting rooms. We declare that all such activity is the work of the Christ who was born to set men free. How we do this in the context of the congregation has a number of very important meanings.

First of all, because the church is an intimate, familiar community in which everything we do obviously affects everyone else, we learn that the recovery of meaning for past, present, and future comes through the body of persons who live in continual encounter with themselves, God, and others. We are more aware all the time how people of this congregation bear up those who are going through a process of personal change in counseling. Dr. Lowell Colston, a pastoral counselor teaching at Christian Theological Seminary, has researched the question of what special benefits come from counseling done

Advent 3: Getting Your History Straight

in a congregational setting. He found that, other things being equal, change in persons was accelerated under conditions of a supporting community with a common faith.[2]

Second, our faith is that we risk what we have said in the arena of life. The pastoral counselor must be involved with those he helps. I know that I cannot expect any magic from the procedures themselves. If I remain aloof and detached while manipulating techniques I will create the same condition in those I see. The orientation the counselor has toward life will be adopted by those who ask his or her help. This means that we who do this work are encouraging a suffering human being to walk forth into the face of calamity. That is an awesome responsibility. In taking it we walk together through a veil of tears into the redemption of Christ. Any therapist who leads someone into such a treacherous path believing *he or she* can save that person by one's own powers has made of oneself an idol. For us here, only the being and activity of God, known in Christ, in the deep caring and rational discipline of the counselor, can heal any wound. For me, it is like Jeremiah: I speak, I cry out,

> I shout, "Violence and destruction!"
> For the word of the Lord has become for me
> a reproach and derision all day long.
> If I say, "I will not mention him, or
> speak any more in his name,"
> there is in my heart as it were a burning fire
> shut up in my bones,
> and I am weary with holding it in,
> and I cannot." (Jer 20:8–9)

Thomas: At this Advent season, this time of preparation for the coming of him who was "born to set the people free," we declare that all the processes of redeeming life from destruction that are to be found in the church and in the world are the work of Christ. They may not be "done in his name." There may be no recognition of his presence and no use of the orthodox

---

2. Hiltner and Colston, *The Context of Pastoral Counseling*.

language of religion. Part of our task is to discover where he is at work, proclaim it, and celebrate it. Another part of our work is to establish the relationships in which his healing ministry may operate most freely and creatively.

The view of life and history revealed in the Bible is linear, directional, purposeful; while so much of what we experience as persons and see all around us in the lives of other persons is cyclical, circular, so that people are bound in fear and depression and failure. How can we possibly escape the conclusion that our mission as ministers of Christ is to break the confining cycles in order that persons may find purpose and direction and meaning, receiving the gifts of joy and hope from the God who sent his Son to set the people free.

Life in such a community of faith is daily experience of death, burial, and resurrection. It is creative encounter with God, self, and others that leads to "getting our history straight"—recovering the meaning of the past, living joyfully in the present, and being hopefully expectant of the future. And possible at all because One was "born to set the people free."

Advent 4: Entering the Main Stream

Keith Watkins and Robert A. Thomas

Thomas: A popular news magazine noted last week that an atmosphere of discouragement pervaded the nation's capital as the ninetieth Congress prepared to adjourn. One senator said of the mood on Capitol Hill:

> It's a tiredness, a frustration, an uneasiness. It's a war with no end in sight. It's a racial and urban problem with no end in sight. It's a fiscal problem with no end in sight. Maybe if we all get out of here, go home and listen to the people for a while, we'll come back with new hope and new ideas and new enthusiasm. But maybe we'll come back more discouraged than ever.[1]

The terrible pressures of life in a revolutionary time are felt in every corner of the land, and recognition of the depth of the issues we face becomes more and more unavoidable. The fact is that social change is reshaping the whole world, not just in a political way but (as George Carpenter says) by cutting away the underlying assumptions of every religion. Faiths are in flux as are tension and radical uncertainty. There is a

---

1. *Time*, December 15, 1967, 23.

"sorting out of identities and relationships that have been long confused." The process is all-pervasive. It ranges from the individual's fundamental faith commitment at one end of the scale, to church-state relations, human rights, and the meaning of freedom at the other end.

In the midst of this process, we are not able to see very clearly what is happening or what the future may be, and we are anxious and afraid. Susanne K. Langer, in her book *Philosophical Sketches*, suggests that later generations will probably see our age as a time of transition from one social order to another, but, she says that "we cannot see the present that way, because what we are moving toward does not yet exist, and we can have no picture of it.... We feel ourselves swept along in a violent passage, from a world we cannot salvage to a world we cannot see; and most people are afraid."[2]

That kind of generalized anxiety and fear is part of our bondage in the modern world. We are having trouble relating to our past, not only "getting our personal history straight," but understanding our tradition as people in the Western world and seeing ourselves as part of an ongoing process that is at the same time conserving and creative.

Here in the United States we have a mixed feeling about the past. On the one hand we are proud of our break with the traditions of Europe, proud of our youth and our freedom to explore and innovate and move ahead in the social structure on the basis of effort and ability. We have little respect for history and we have rewarded the powers and enthusiasms of youth far more than we have reverenced the knowledge and wisdom of the elders. On the other hand, there is a sense in which we are almost idolatrous about our tradition. Patriotism becomes increasingly potent as a motivation for life; people like the "old-time religion"; universities become more and more conservative in nature, though now and then a radical professor makes the headlines. We are not sure whether tradition stifles and weakens persons and societies

---

2. Langer, *Philosophical Sketches*, 141.

Advent 4: Entering the Main Stream

or frees and empowers them. Nor have we been able to decide how to find our proper freedom.

Watkins: The past can shackle us. This power to stifle creativity, to subject us to the visions of the dead, is the substance of a passionate statement on architecture by Frank Lloyd Wright. When sixteen years old, after reading Victor Hugo's account of the decline of architecture in the West, he saw "the Renaissance as that setting sun all Europe mistook for dawn." A short time later, as he watched construction under way, the new west wing of the state capitol in Madison, Wisconsin, collapsed, carrying forty men to their death in a blinding cloud of lime dust. The classic cornice, which had been "projecting boldly out from the top of the building, against the sky," was now revealed as fake, as "great hollow boxes of galvanized iron." Caught by his foot beneath this cornice, hanging head downward, was one of the workmen. It was, says Wright, "early disillusionment and cruel, this vision of the lifeblood of idolized architecture ebbing slowly away.... If the old order is to be preserved—regardless—it is not well for boys to read the great poets, nor see classic buildings fall down."[3]

This drive to preserve the old order is what shackles the human spirit and condemns a culture to death. The power of death is at work in American politics whenever the rural mentality of the nineteenth century frontier continues to dominate, binding cities so tightly that they cannot care for the opportunities and desperate needs of their people. One can see it in the university whenever a militant positivism or frozen liberalism perpetuates a proud disdain of religion in the name of intellectual freedom. One can see this power in the church. The Curia, which has represented the preservation of the old order regardless, has sought to destroy the rising tide of reform in the Roman Catholic Church. Reactionaries in the United Presbyterian Church, who are determined to fight once more the battles of the sixteenth century, are doing their best to shackle that great American denomination. Supporters of

---

3. Wright, *The Future of Architecture*, 125, 127.

the Atlanta Declaration have tried to do the same thing among the Disciples of Christ. The old guard of every congregation of every denomination stifle new life and bind the hands and hearts and voices of those who would move forward.

Thomas: This effort to preserve the old order is one of the most powerful forces operating at any time—which means that there are two factors at work: one of them is an understanding of the basis of personal and cultural life; the other is a distortion of this basis, which, because of its twisted form, destroys rather than supports life. For our personal health as well as the vitality of our culture, we must try to sort out the genuine from the distorted. We must distinguish between Tradition as a living stream and the traditions which are its momentary expressions.

Watkins: To do so, we should begin with a level of life familiar to all of us. Every family has a unique character which sets it apart from every other family. The distinctiveness has to do not with details but with intangibles: mood, attitudes, convictions, the style with which details of eating and sleeping and skirmishing with one another are carried out. It has to do with the subtle ties connecting husband and wife, parents and children, brothers and sisters. When you visit in the house where the family lives, and listen to the sounds, and feel with the sensors of the spirit, you can detect the mystique which characterizes the family more than anything else. Change the details of family life, move it from one house to another, add a child by birth, subtract another by marriage, alter income, hamper the people by old age, and yet that intangible quality is still there.

What is true of a family is also true of a city, a nation, a culture: there is an inner mood or conviction, a perception of life's meaning which expresses itself in systems of thought and styles of art, political and social institutions, ethical theories and patterns of personal life. Yet the spirit or living center of the community is something other than these particular forms which clothe it. The United States of America is a living tradition, partially expressed by political alliances. Yet America

Advent 4: Entering the Main Stream

today is the America of former years even though the Federalist Party, the Republican Party of Jefferson, the Whigs and the "Know Nothings" and the "Bull Moosers" and the "Dixiecrats" have all come into existence and then vanished away.

So it is with the Christian faith. Theologians speak of Tradition, with a capital T, and traditions with a lower-case t. The one is that living stream which flows on through all of the passing systems and forms; the other is the constantly changing series of partial expressions, the outmoded theologies, ephemeral moralities. Christian Tradition is a vision of meaning in the face of absurdity, a conviction of purpose in the natural order seemingly devoid of reason, a certainty that individual life makes sense despite the despair which so easily besets us. It comes to its fullest form in the man who came to live among us, demonstrating by his own life how purpose is present even when the powers of this order conspire to destroy all that is good.

This Tradition, more than any other force, has shaped the institutions, the intellectual forces and ethical theories, the undergirding fabric of trust and selflessness and care for others which we in the Western world take for granted. From our birth onward we have been thrust into this stream for it flows through the very way of life which each of us lives in the first decades of our existence.

The greatest danger facing us at any moment is that we confuse something temporary with the living stream of Tradition itself. What can happen is that a partial form, a tradition with lower-case t, is accepted as Tradition with capital T, and we waste our energies trying to maintain it. We slip into a stagnant pool of quiet water, like the Columbia River Slough in the lowlands north of Portland, thinking that we are in the main stream of the Columbia River. By staying in the slough, we miss that last powerful lunge of the river toward its destiny in the Pacific. We swim, but with the carp rather than the salmon. Those who protect the cornice, whose liberalism is frozen in the late nineteenth century, who perpetuate the "old time religion," are in the slough, and the river goes on without them. Life comes when we leave the slough and enter the main stream.

Thomas: But how does anyone know anything about the destiny toward which the stream of Tradition moves? Where are the clues, the touchstones? Isn't Susanne Langer right when she says that the "old metaphors have lost their aptness, the old models broken, and humanity—especially the most sensitive and thoughtful part of humanity everywhere—has lost its mental orientation and moral certitude?"[4]

Watkins: What Langer says is true. We do not yet see what the new world will be. Yet there are clues—some of which come from the past. In all the history of the race there have been very few radical changes in the foundation which supports human life, and one of these came in the fourth century of the Common Era. The glories of Greece, transmuted by the military might and organizing genius of Rome had supported the whole structure of life, personal and public. People interpreted themselves and the world, and their place in it, by means of the cosmic myth and ethical principles growing out of the ancient past. But these spiritual structures no longer compelled belief, no longer satisfied the inner longings of people, no longer dealt with the confusions which confronted that "world come of age."

What came to pass in the fourth century was the creation of a new basis for personal and public life. In the monasteries in the desert, in the palaces of emperors, in the apses of new basilican churches, in the centers of learning, in the homes of common people this new foundation was forged. It was wrought from varied material: Hellenistic thought and oriental mysticism, Hebraic perceptions of historical meaning, Germanic vitality and Roman order—all cemented together by the faith which Jesus of Nazareth created in human hearts. For a millennium and a half this new social order has endured, supporting most of the cultural achievements which we accept without question as the proper inheritance of humankind.

---

4. Langer, *Philosophical Sketches*, 145.

Advent 4: Entering the Main Stream

Our own generation is entering a period very much like the fourth century. Interpreters point to the fact that the cohesion of Western culture is no longer strong enough to hold together the powerful forces which are now building up. Already technological civilization has swept the globe so that even the most primitive people can no longer continue the simple life of their past. Ancient cultural traditions are regathering strength and competing with one another as were the ancient faiths in the fourth century. All around us, and in us, there is rising a new culture which will embrace all humankind just as the culture created in the fourth century embraced the Mediterranean Basin. The dividing walls are being broken down and a new human life more expansive than anything ever to exist is coming into being. This is the direction that the main stream is heading. The surge of the waters is toward this destiny.

Thomas: We are the disciples of one who was "born to set the people free." He did not disregard his heritage, nor was he unaware of his Tradition. He spoke of his life as a fulfillment of the Law rather than as its destruction. But he had no respect for the particularities of the tradition (with a small t). While he deliberately challenged the legalisms which destroyed the spirit of the Law, his word and work were revelation of the universals of the Tradition. God's eternal love for his creation, and his intention to bring it to fulfillment, were made clear in the "Christ-Event." People were set free from bondage to particularities by a new vision of the universal.

So in our time, when all the anchors seem to be coming loose, when an upheaval in history is occurring that seems more drastic than anything people have known before, when no one can see a picture of what the future will be, our need is for awareness of the reality of the deep-running stream of Tradition made known in the present work of Christ in the world. The particularities of racial and sectarian and national traditions are not worthy of final devotion; only the great universals deserve our respect and commitment.

We are children of particular traditions, of course; national, racial, and denominational. And we do not desert the values each may uphold. But the first allegiance of our lives cannot be to any of our separatist traditions. Our first loyalty is to that Tradition behind and within the movements of history that liberates, unifies, and reconciles the whole life of humankind. And it is just because of our faith in the reality of that "main stream" that we are able to live in such a time of radical change with hope. Once we feel our lives are in that stream and that we are being carried along toward a future that is greater and better than any people in the past have known, we are set free to engage creatively and with joy in whatever new kinds of institutional and extra-institutional expressions of the universals that seem to hold the possibilities of life for humankind. We are no longer bound by the past, wasting our energy defending the particularities that are dead, but men and women who can live in this "world come of age" exercising our true humanity and rejoicing in "the time to come."

Advent 5: Delivered

Robert A. Thomas

Suffering people in every age and land have longed for deliverance. Even when their circumstances have offered no ground for hope, they have continued to hope. The capacity to keep on living and striving is one of humanity's most extraordinary characteristics; it may, indeed, be the awakening point of religious awareness, the beginning place of faith. The hope of salvation, of deliverance, in one form or another, is always part of religion, and when there has seemed no basis for hope for worldly well-being, men and women have sought "a salvation not made with hands" from some realm beyond earthly existence.

Twenty-five hundred years ago pre-Confucian Chinese peasants complained about harsh tax collectors in this song:

> Big rat, big rat,
> Do not eat my millet!
> Three years have I served you,
> But you will not care for me.
> I am going to leave you
> And go to that happy land;
> Happy land, happy land,
> Where I will find my place.

And scarcely more than a hundred years ago Negro slaves in America sang:

Advent Dialogues: Born to Set the People Free

> Roll, Jordan, roll!
> Roll, Jordan, roll!
> I'm goin' to go to heaven when I die,
> To hear old Jordan roll!

George Carpenter suggests that a number of religions of the world are "religions of escape," including all the forms of primitive Animism, Hinduism, Buddhism, and "Introverted Christianity." He believes that escapist salvation-seeking is characteristic of a part of Christianity from the beginning, and that it has all too often vitiated the life and witness of the church.

> In the early centuries some ardent Christians felt impelled to go out alone into the desert to wrestle with their sins, instead of bearing their part in society and in the corporate fellowship of the church. Through the centuries Christians have tried to assure their own salvation by rigorous moralism, by ascetic practices, even by the pursuit of martyrdom. Neither the practices themselves nor the idea of gaining salvation thereby find any warrant in the New Testament, but anxiety to escape the imagined terrors of hell and gain the felicity of heaven has often been the dominant motive of Christian preaching. To cleric and layman alike, this was what the gospel was about. Little else mattered.[1]

While the hope of salvation in one way or another has always been part of religion, and while the term "salvation" always includes the idea of release from threat or danger or burden, it is closely related to the more general term "liberation." The one way of using the word emphasizes the notion of safety; the other emphasizes the concept of freedom. Although there may be a sense in which "safety" and "freedom" go together, there is a division in Christianity at exactly this point. There is, as Carpenter says, a type of Christianity which is self-seeking, escapist, introverted. Its concern is with "safety-salvation," not with "freedom-salvation." A kind of religion which tends to isolate the individual in a world of private concern, it is apt to be pietistic, puritanical, and legalistic. It is not interested

---

1. Carpenter, *Encounter of the Faiths*, 53. The two songs in the preceding paragraph are quoted by Carpenter on 33.

Advent 5: Delivered

in freeing people to live *in* the world, but in rescuing them *from* the world.

The presupposition of this sermon series is that Christ was born to set the people free and that this concern for the coming of people to their full humanity was not something new in the creation, but another and deeply moving evidence of God's purpose from the beginning.

> When all things began, the Word already was. The Word dwelt with God, and what God was, the Word was.... All that came to be was alive with his life, and that life was the light of men. The light shines on in the dark, and the darkness has never quenched it.... So the Word became flesh; he came to dwell among us, and we saw his glory, such glory as befits the Father's only Son, full of grace and truth. (John 1:1–14 NEB)

That was the testimony of the author of the Fourth Gospel, and it is for all people. Whenever people have seen light, known love, sought the fullness of their humanity, given themselves for the sake of others, suffered for truth, rejoiced in beauty, there the Word has been at work.

That Word, that creative power and love of God, became visible flesh and blood in Jesus Christ. That's the meaning of the incarnation. And that event is the basis of Christian faith. But it does not stand all by itself. It is an event with a history not only poetically and philosophically described by John, but alluded to by the author of the Gospel according to Luke in the narrative of the birth of Jesus, and especially in the song of Zechariah, father of John the Baptist.

> Praise to the God of Israel!
> For he has turned to his people, saved them and set them free,
> and has raised up a deliverer of victorious power
> from the house of his servant David
> So he promised: age after age he proclaimed
> by the lips of his holy prophets
> that he would deliver us from our enemies,
> out of the hands of all who hate us;
> that he would deal mercifully with our fathers,
> calling to mind his solemn covenant.

> Such was the oath he swore to our father Abraham,
> to rescue us from enemy hands,
> and grant us, free from fear, to worship him
> with a holy worship, with uprightness of heart,
> in his presence, our whole life long.
> And you, my child, you shall be called Prophet of the Highest,
> for you will be the Lord's forerunner, to prepare his way
> and lead his people to salvation through knowledge of him
> by the forgiveness of their sins:
> for in the tender compassion of our God
> the morning sun from heaven will rise upon us.
> to shine on those who live in darkness, under the cloud of death,
> and to guide our feet into the way of peace.
> (Luke 1:68–79)

Luke composed this song as a companion piece to "the Magnificat." In many cases he used one half of a verse from the Psalms in Mary's hymns of praise of the early church, lifting up the personal joy of their singers into much larger realms. One is reminded of Israel's history, beginning with Abraham's leaving the land of his fathers and God's promise to him and to the world through him. It was that covenant with Abraham, confirmed by the deliverance of the Hebrews out of Egypt under Moses and their establishment in Palestine as a nation, that gave their history meaning. It was as the Deliverer from bondage that priests and prophets and psalmists proclaimed God. It was in terms of a reciprocal covenant obligating Israel to worship God in return for the liberty and security of the nation that the idea of mutual responsibility between God and humanity took root. In the earliest times Israel looked for material deliverance from the slavery in Egypt, the captivity in Babylon, the military power of her neighbors. But the hope for the future was gradually refined and spiritually deepened by the noblest representatives of the "chosen people." Under the impact of historical experience, and deepening appreciation of the human condition, and the inspiration of the prophets the expected deliverance came to relate more to moral and spiritual values. Victory achieved by the sword came to be felt as nothing in comparison with victory achieved by patient endurance of wrong. Deliverance from the enemy was conceived a poor salvation if unaccompanied by deliverance from sin.

By the time of Isaiah, deliverance from idolatry, and the destruction of war and sin and death are the chief marks of the Messianic Age to come. And by the time of Jeremiah and Joel, the gift of God to humankind is described in terms of the transformation of the inner spirit, the creation of a new covenant written not on tablets of clay or stone but on human hearts, so that obedience to God is the result of a spontaneous expression of an inward communion with God resting on God's will, knowledge of which has become the common possession of all (Jer 31:31–34).

> And it shall come to pass afterward,
> that I will pour out my spirit on all flesh;
> your sons and your daughters shall prophesy,
> your old men shall dream dreams
> and your young men shall see visions. (Joel 2:28)

So Israel's hope for deliverance and expectation for the future changed, and the "Deliverer," once seen as a king prancing upon his war horse, appeared to the purged eyes of later times as "one meek and lowly of heart riding upon an ass." This does not mean the old earthly materialistic hopes of conquest, victory, and dominion were forever laid low. Far from it! They have always been with us, sometimes obliterating and sometimes blended with those nobler ideals and values that were achieved in the process of the ages.

All this is to help us see that Luke's references to deliverance and a "deliverer" have historical antecedents, and Christianity's understanding of Jesus as one who saves—who delivers—was not plucked out of thin air. The "God of Abraham, Isaac and Jacob" is the God who creates and redeems, who acts in history as One who delivers, and strangely manifests himself in the birth of a baby.

> And so it was, that, while they were there, the days were accomplished that she should be delivered. And she brought forth her firstborn son, and wrapped him in swaddling clothes, and laid him in a manger; because there was no room for them in the inn. (Luke 2:6–7)

Advent Dialogues: Born to Set the People Free

The baby Jesus was born as all human infants are born; brought into the world by a mother's pain, the fetus liberated from the mother's body, freed from the confinement of the womb, the umbilical cord cut so as to make it possible for the person to be a person, separate and distinct from all others. From darkness and warmth and absolute dependence, from unconsciousness and irresponsibility, the baby was delivered into a world whose inns were full so that only mangers were available for resting places, a world in which a Herod could order babies slaughtered, and people know how to build crosses to torture and kill their fellows.

But a world so full of the creative power of God as to make possible the love of fathers and mothers for their children, the growth of a lad in "wisdom and stature and favor with God and man" and a deepening awareness of the Eternal; a world in which the achievement of a full humanity was possible and the commitment of life to the purposes of God so complete as to make that life seem transparent and God himself visible. The baby Jesus was delivered into the world by his mother, but in a larger sense by the creative force of the universe, by God.

Deliverance is always from something to something. In the case of the baby Jesus it was from absolute dependence, darkness, and physical restraint to light and growth and possible personhood, to learning and choice and responsibility; from being delivered to becoming deliverer! Suffering and pain were involved in both cases; his mother's first and then his own. It may always be true that deliverance comes through the effort, suffering, and devotion of persons. But in the larger sense it always comes from God.

In this series of sermons we have spoken of many of the ways in which people of our time are bound, restrained, imprisoned. We have described our present need of deliverance from fear and selfishness and pride and death. We have looked at the ways people seek deliverance from their bondage and how they turn from the heritage of faith and hope that is in our Tradition because of superficial understanding or mistaking the sloughs for the mainstream. Those in the mainstream know that deliverance has come. God has acted in history. We point to a series of those 'mighty acts' as evidence of the work and purpose of a Deliverer, and in particular to

Advent 5: Delivered

the Christ-event with its dramatic proclamation of God's redeeming love.

But the Christian witness is not only to some events, or an event of past history. It is to Christ's work in the present, the delivery of men and women from anxiety and fear, from loneliness and boredom, from futility and nihilism, from isolation and separation, to light and creativity and full humanity. In our own time persons are being delivered from the cycles of destruction and death in their personal history into a purposeful life, breaking out of fears and failures and depression. Young people are discovering the wonder of God's gift of love and trust and responding in joy with a commitment of themselves. Communities—congregations—accept the gift of freedom and are enabled to see their work and mission with new clarity and depth and thus find themselves in the midst of a process of renewal and reconciliation. The Deliverer is at work!

Deliverance in our experience comes through the effort, suffering, and devotion of persons, but in the larger sense that deliverance always comes from God. The suffering of God is not finished. The labor of God is not done. We are being delivered from the prisons of darkness and fear and death to become free persons, loving human beings, living in communities of love. The God of Abraham, Isaac, and Jacob is the God of Jesus Christ, is the God of the people of this time, and is the God of the future that is to be. We have been bound, but we are being delivered by One "born to set the people free!"

Lenten Dialogues:
The Tragic Vision

Lent 1: In Sight of the City He Wept

Robert A. Thomas

The season of preparation for Easter, which may historically have been the Christian adaptation of springtime celebrations of awakening in pre-Christian cultures, is called Lent and includes the forty-day period (excluding Sundays) before Easter Day. And even though the people of our free church tradition have carefully avoided subservience to a "Church Year" with its prescribed festivals and holy days, we have shared with practically all the branches of the church this time of special teaching and encouragement, of personal penitence and discipline in the hope of renewal for individuals and institutions.

The readings from the Scripture and the sermons during this season encourage introspection in the light of the gospel of the crucified and risen Lord. There is often an alternation between consideration of events in Christ's life and events in our own. Everywhere one observes a wider participation in study and worship, a more serious effort to grapple with the meanings of Christian faith and the styles of Christian life.

In the past generation there has been a re-awakening of the tragic sense of life after a long period of superficial optimism in which a variety of "gospels of modernity" promised to resolve all the vast

Lenten Dialogues: The Tragic Vision

contradictions of life by means of some simple scheme of science or education. Joining the poets and dramatists and disillusioned philosophers and writers have been many theologians and serious adherents of the Christian faith, making common cause against the sentimentality of former generations, vigorously attacking that delusive optimism which held that goodness always triumphs.

The events of our time and the conditions in which we find ourselves, with all their improbables and fluidity, force serious people toward a tragic vision of life. We speak of every step we take as "the calculated risk." Nowhere are there any guarantees of security and no one dares promise any immediate renovation of our present disorder, either the urban crisis or the Vietnam War. Hordes of refugees live in a special type of misery, an additional quarter million of them created in the last month. Without citizenship and in exile, we call them "displaced persons." But Nathan Scott has pointed out that we are all "displaced persons," who cannot find anywhere a satisfactory dwelling place in the world of our time. There is outer disorder plainly visible to everyone, but the inner world of the private self is just as troubled by fear, remorse, and sometimes hysteria. "The ancient issues of tragedy," he says, "are reinstated with a new kind of urgency."[1]

The people whose vision is of the tragic cast are preoccupied by these facts of human existence. Their focus is on the background of danger against which the human drama must be enacted; the circumstances and situations, the forces and powers in the midst of which choices must be made and life lived. They are aware of what Paul Tillich called the "boundary situations" of human existence, where people are nakedly exposed and the limitations and imperfections of their creatureliness can be no longer hid from view.

While it is true that the final accent of the Christian proclamation is *not* on tragedy, but on hope and victory, it is just as true that there is no significant note of hope that does not take account of our condition as it really is, the world without and within, the suffering and sickness of humankind. Christians have to take seriously the passion of Jesus, the pain and anguish of our Lord, its evidence of

---

1. Scott, *The Tragic Vision*, xv.

Lent 1: In Sight of the City He Wept

the God who himself suffers and thereby accomplishes our deliverance. Too much of our prayer and worship is an escape, taking us away from the real concerns of life into a world of make-believe and inaction. Such prayer and worship may yield a comforting illusion, as John Macquarrie suggests, "but the price paid for this illusion is that the believer is prevented from entering fully either into the enjoyment of the pathos of a truly human existence."[2]

The tragic sense of life is not alien to Christian faith. As Scott puts it, "the penultimate event in the Christian story—Calvary—can be made no sense of at all apart from the kind of perception the tragedian seeks to assist us in attaining." Only those who have accepted a "vocation to tragedy" can understand the whole point and meaning of Job's declaration, "I know that my redeemer liveth," or the full poignancy and gloriousness of Paul's word, "If God be for us, who can be against us?"[3]

We rob ourselves of the depth of meaning in Christian faith, the full joy of affirmation and commitment, when we are unwilling to confront in all its stark tragedy the gospel account of the closing days of Jesus' ministry, seeing in it the revelation of humanity's best and worst, life's terrible and glorious realities: God.[4] At worst, that leaves us with human actors obeying the decrees of God so that they had no responsibility or guilt.

Whatever we think of the interpretations of the first Christians, it is clear that the church's faith was particularly concerned with this piece of tradition. It was the center of preaching and teaching. The problem for us now, twenty centuries later, is to weigh the various interpretations of New Testament authors (for there are more than one), set them alongside what we can discover of ancient history from other sources, exercise caution and critical judgment regarding details of the story, and face the fact, as Bornkamm puts it, that "all we can recognize are outlines of the course of events of the last week."[5]

---

2. Macquarrie, *God and Secularity*, 47.
3. Scott, *The Tragic Vision*, xii.
4. Bornkamm, *Jesus of Nazareth*, 156.
5. Bornkamm, *Jesus of Nazareth*, 157.

Lenten Dialogues: The Tragic Vision

Success and failure, popularity and enmity had been part and parcel of Jesus' ministry from the start. At the beginning he had rejected a political interpretation of his mission and he never was able to get his disciples to understand. He went to Jerusalem for a final judgment on that mission, to deliver the message of the coming kingdom of God in the city which he himself called "the city of the Great King." That decision was the turning point in his life. Later tradition makes it seem as though he only went there to seek his death, to fulfill the prophecies. But modern interpreters of Jesus believe he went to confront the people in the holy city with the message of the kingdom of God and to summon them at the eleventh hour to make their decision. He had to go to Jerusalem; it was not only the capital city, but also the place connected from ancient times with Israel's destiny. We can't know when he came to the realization of his own possible and violent end, nor can we know at what moment his readiness to accept death turned into the certainty of it. But there can be no doubt that he knew the road to Jerusalem led to new and serious conflict with the religious and temporal rulers.

It is probable that Jesus had been to Jerusalem many times, and even possible that he had worked at his ministry there. Maurice Goguel, in his great *Life of Jesus* published in Paris in 1932, developed the theory that Jesus spent the closing months of the year 27 in Jerusalem, where he was disappointed in the misunderstanding that greeted him. He gained some disciples and the general sympathy of the masses but aroused the hostility of the authorities so that he had to leave the city and withdraw to Perea. There he spent another three months with his disciples, and then came back to Jerusalem for the final few days, hoping when he returned that the masses would greet him boldly and he would be able to brave the opposition of the priests. Goguel believed that sequence of events best fits the Gospel accounts and the sense of meaning they convey. I find it a powerful thesis, and particularly his placing the story of Jesus' weeping over the city at the point when he left it to go to Perea rather than when he approached it on what we call Palm Sunday. That is possible because in Matthew and Mark almost the same words are in a different setting (Matt 23:37–39).

Lent 1: In Sight of the City He Wept

Whenever it was uttered, that lamentation over the city must have been at the spot in the road from Jerusalem to Bethany that winds around the southeast slope of the Mount of Olives. There is a place where the whole city is spread out before the traveler, the ancient walls are surrounding the Dome of the Rock which stands where the temple once stood, and the streets and houses clearly visible all around. "In sight of the city, he wept." How could he help it? He loved Jerusalem. It was a delight to the eye, for its history wherein Isaiah and Jeremiah had walked its streets, for its associations with the Scriptures he loved, and because it was the "city of the Great King"—God's chosen as his voice and hand. Neither Jesus nor any other Jew could see its temple from a distance without a stirring of the soul.

But Jesus wept because that city's history had been one long and tragic dirge of radiant hopes unrealized, vast possibilities unfilled. Time and again national disaster had followed disregard of the pleading of prophet and priest, and even then the heel of tyrant boot rankled patriot heart. Jesus wept because his disciples misunderstood, the people still refused to heed the message of the kingdom, and the history of the city promised nothing better. "O Jerusalem, Jerusalem, the city that murders the prophets and stones the messengers sent to her! How often have I longed to gather your children as a hen gathers her brood under her wings; but you would not let me" (Matt 23:37).

Jerusalem, "the city of peace," could not see when its true peace came! Jesus took that as a sign of the times, "because you did not recognize God's moment when it came" there was nothing ahead but siege and destruction, "not one stone standing on another." The tears of Jesus are the tears of tragedy; his love for Jerusalem is in tension with his acceptance of its judgment. He was confident he could save Jerusalem; beneath his sadness there was the conviction that Jerusalem could have a different history if it would but turn to the kingdom. But his hope burned low, if now it flamed at all.

Is that not the way God sees our cities today? Their superficiality and materialism are everywhere evident, as is their refusal to learn from history. Still Jesus suffers as destructive forces hold sway and the powerful protect their kingdoms and the institutions of religion continue in the habits and practices of the past. Still he weeps as the ghettos grow more crowded, and the hatreds spread, and the congressional committees make their reports, and the evidence piles up that the white man really doesn't care enough. "In sight of the city, he wept." Every moment is a moment of crisis, of judgment or consolation, a moment for turning, "God's moment." Christ still weeps, and still hopes, and God still intends the kingdom.

Lent 2: His Hand with Mine on the Table

Keith Watkins and Robert A. Thomas

Thomas: Every serious Christian confronts a division in his own house. Being human, we possess a certain will-to-power. Our biological heritage protects and insures that will-to-live, that desire-to-exist, even at the expense of the existence of others. We are the product of a struggle for life that is visible in the history and pre-history of mankind. These forces are still part of our life; civilization has not destroyed them, as anyone who examines his own life or looks underneath the surface of the life around us, is well aware. The drives and powers are redirected in our time into socially approved channels in which the welfare and safety of the community is protected or enhanced. We are conditioned to achieve in the production of goods or services, directing our physical and psychic energies toward winning material wealth and power, thus satisfying those primal, powerful forces in the competitive worlds of business or politics or education. In economic life it becomes ever clearer that the chief reward and satisfaction for many people is power over the lives of others. Once they achieve a certain material wealth, additional wealth is no longer very meaningful. It is power that satisfies, and ever-increasing power that is the goal.

This will to achieve, to become a success, to gain wealth and power, to seek one's own place in the sun, whether or not it is characteristic of all people everywhere, is certainly characteristic of modern Americans. One sees that drive for power in the life of every social institution, whether ecclesiastical, academic, political, or economic, and at nearly every level of its life. One sees it, even, in the life of one's family and in the various kinds of social groups to which one belongs. Church members, persons committed to the gospel, have always been uneasy at the direct confrontation in their own lives of the existence and power of these inner drives that seem to be native to our humanity. We read of One who went about "doing good," who seemed to care little for his own physical needs and advised his disciples to give their attention to other matters first. We hear sermons about being "a servant people" from ministers who seem to have no understanding of our economic and social system and themselves are exercising a will-to-live and a will-to-power without giving much evidence of being aware of it. We are drawn to the One who lived for others, but the more we think about living for others ourselves, the more impossibly idealistic it appears.

And even when we are trying to relate our lives meaningfully to the church, when we believe that God has revealed himself in Jesus Christ, when we are convinced that the way of love is the way of hope for humankind, we are still driven by that desire to lord it over others. Our life may be a wavering back and forth, a selfish striving after success—wealth and power—part of the time, and a sudden stopping short to consider meanings and values of another kind at other times. Some of us never make a firm commitment; others of us change courses along the way and shift directions. None of us can be serious about our lives without recognizing the power and forces that exist in us and being poignantly aware of the ambiguity of what we do.

Israel's history, much of it focusing in the life of Jesus of Nazareth and narrowing down even more pointedly in the last days of his life, witnesses to the power of these human drives, the terrible choices people are called upon to make, and the tragic confusion and ambiguity of the motivations and deeds of even the best-intentioned people.

Watkins: Jesus and his disciples revealed the will-to-power in their own lives when they worked for the restoration of David's kingdom. A thousand years had elapsed since David had lifted his tribes to prominence in the political and military affairs of his time. Although Israel's golden age didn't last long, the hope of its return inspired patriots for a thousand years. They dreamed of a new king, a messiah, who would throw off the yoke of bondage and recapture the greatness that once had been theirs.

Some saw the messiah as "a pre-existent, heavenly angelic being who, at the end of time, [would] appear at the side of God as judge of the world."[1] Others believed that he would be a man descended from David who would rise up to lead the nation to empire as had David long before. Many of Jesus' contemporaries supported this nationalistic, militaristic version of the messianic vision. These Zealots, as they were called, were revolutionaries, guerillas, conspirators who organized and trained and prepared for the violent overthrow of Roman domination. Some of the disciples had been Zealots. Judas Iscariot may have been one. There is evidence that Jesus himself may have sympathized with their views and for a time understood his own ministry as leading to the recovery of national independence and grandeur. Even during the final period of his life, his warnings had that ring. He spoke of "signs in sun and moon and stars," of "distress of nations," of the "shaking of the powers of heaven," of seeing "the Son of man coming in a cloud with power and great glory," of their "redemption drawing near."

---

1. Jenni, "Messiah, Jewish" in Buttrick et al., *Interpreter's Dictionary of the Bible*, 364.

Lenten Dialogues: The Tragic Vision

The religious tradition of Israel developed a second motif, the Suffering Servant, who stood in sharp contrast to the kingly messiah. He was understood to be the chosen one, just as was the messiah, but at this point the similarity ended. The Suffering Servant was to work quietly in order to accomplish his purpose. He would willingly bear disfigurement and violence. He would suffer for the wrongdoing of others and by his own pain bring healing to those for whom he bore it. Some of the Old Testament songs about the servant give the impression that he would be a specific person who someday would fulfill these qualities. In other passages, the servant seems to be the whole nation of Israel whom God would use to accomplish his will among the nations.

But whether the vision was of a single servant or of a servant nation, the qualities of that one were always the same. He would be despised and rejected by the people, a man of sorrows, and acquainted with grief, wounded, bruised, oppressed, rejected—and all for the sake of the people whom he came to serve but who turned away from him.

Thomas: There is good reason to believe that Jesus carried about both images—kingly messiah and Suffering Servant—wavering first toward the one and then toward the other. It may have been that the early part of his ministry was characterized by emphasis upon the popular messianic expectation. Yet, the popular uprising did not come, the great leap forward did not take place, there was no great response to his word, and he retired for a while during which time the servant motif seems to have become dominant. He came back to the city prepared to suffer whatever might come, convinced now that this was the way God had chosen.

Watkins: By Thursday when he sat at table with his closest followers, the issue was resolved in his own mind. Messiah and Suffering Servant were one and the same, but the servant motif was dominant. By his suffering for the people he would usher in a new kingdom, but one of the spirit rather than of imperial power. This resolution of his own inner struggle is very

Lent 2: His Hand with Mine on the Table

clear in the events of the meal. As host, he led these men in the ancient table ceremonies of his people. Picking up a loaf of bread, he prayed: "Blessed art thou, O King of the World, who bringest forth bread from the earth." He said these words fully conscious of the coming crisis—when at the hands of his own people he would suffer. The picture which would come to mind, says Rudolf Otto, was that of stoning, a literal breaking open of the body by people goaded to fury. "The taking, breaking, crunching, crumbling of bread constitutes the most dramatic analogy to the breaking of the body." At this point, Jesus altered the prescribed ceremony by adding a new meaning to the traditional action. "This is my body."

After his death, looking back on this last meal with Jesus, the disciples began to understand what must have been in his mind. The giving of himself into the hands of the enemy was a deliberate act of self-sacrifice. What he did, he did of his own free will—and it was for them. In ways they could only dimly comprehend, their life was now radically different because of Jesus' giving of himself over to suffering and death.

Thomas: This episode, with its conflict of motives and premonitions of suffering, is at the same time marked by a sense of hope. How can this be? How can anyone claim that good will come from the disaster which so often besets us?

Watkins: These two elements—disaster and hope—must both be present for an event to be tragic. Great tragedy, as Charles G. Bell points out, springs "from a ground of earthly pessimism, but it rises in the conviction of human worth and the divine splendour of things." The right blend of these qualities is rarely present, and the tragic sense easily gives way to a whine which may hurt but which lacks a sense of grandeur. In great tragedy there is a redemption, says, Bell, but of a special kind, and contrasts Shakespeare and Ibsen to show what he means. It is not that one says that life is good and the other says that it is a "morbid waste." Instead, Shakespeare says that "life is a walking shadow" while Ibsen stresses that it "should be the heart's desire." Yet "Shakespeare can put his characters through

85

violence and wasteful death and bring them out living souls," while Ibsen "crushes life out of his in a universe which has no value apart from that romantic span which they have been denied." Great tragedy, Bell concludes, consumes "programmatic defeat in some flame of tacit and spiritual victory."[2]

This kind of tragic vision is what we see portrayed in Jesus' last meal before death. Crushed are the dreams of empire; destroyed are the ambitions for power; broken is the triumphalism of the Zealot dream. In their place is explicit and programmatic defeat. Yet there is redemption which, to use another of Bell's phrases, "burns like a godhead" through the close of this somber episode.

Thomas: Certainly this kind of tragic vision was present in Jesus' mind as he broke the bread and passed around the cup of wine. And in time to come, it was present among Christians when they renewed this meal as the central act of their worship. For the disciples that night, however, the ambiguity was still unresolved. Dreams of power and privilege still dominated their minds, as is evident in the Lukan account with its juxtaposition of betrayal and support.

Watkins: During the evening Jesus announced that there was a betrayer among them—"his hand with mine on the table." How much Jesus knew about Judas' intentions, how much the disciples knew about each other's mixture of motives, is not related to us. All that is recorded is that they began to ask among themselves who it might be who could do such a thing. Nor do we know why Judas had determined upon his course of action. Was it for so simple a reason as greed? Or was it because of frustrated hopes? Maybe he was a Zealot, determined to protect the honor of the divine law, first seeing in Jesus the Messiah who could overthrow Rome, but now disillusioned because the "lion of the tribe of Judah" had become a sheep unwilling to go through with it after all.

At this point in the story, when all attention is focused upon the betrayer, Luke introduces what he calls the zealous

2. Bell, "Tragedy," 12–32.

dispute about rank and privilege: who of them would have the highest positions in the kingdom which Christ would establish? At first reading, nothing could be in sharper contrast to betrayal than the earning of high rank because of loyalty. Jesus, however, turned the matter around in such a way that this very talk of rank became a form of betrayal. For, the disciples did not understand Jesus' decision about the future; they misconstrued the events that were taking place; they failed to see the basis of relationship which Jesus was advocating; they confused privilege with favor and power with faithfulness. For them the messiah motif, with its dreams of empire, still dominated. They did not yet realize that the leader would win his way by suffering. To the degree that their misunderstandings motivated them, they were thus betraying Jesus as much as was Judas with his overt traitor's kiss. Jesus' words make it clear:

> In the world, kings lord it over their subjects; and those in authority are called their country's "Benefactors." Not so with you; on the contrary, the highest among you must bear himself like the youngest, the chief of you like a servant. For who is greater—the one who sits at table or the servant who waits on him? Surely the one who sits at table. Yet here am I among you like a servant. (Luke 22:25–27)

John records that during this meal Jesus departed from his role as host by taking a towel and basin of water and washing the feet of his disciples. In this way his talk of waiting on them like a servant came into full view. And so it must be for us.

Thomas: Two meanings of all this seem to stand clear. The first is that we are faced with a fundamental choice about the direction of our lives. We determine to put first the seeking of wealth, power, and control over the lives of others, or we determine that the first thing in our lives will be the recognition of the meaning and value and needs of others, and our responsibility to serve. We all choose whether we will interpret life from our particular and self-centered will-to-live and will-to-power over the lives of others, or we determine that the first thing in our lives will be the recognition of the meaning and value and needs of others, and our responsibility to serve. All of us decide whether we will interpret life from our particular and self-centered will-to-live and will-to-power, or whether we will interpret life from the view of its opportunities to live with others, share in the common tasks, and take the servant stance. That choice faced Jesus and he forced it upon his disciples by his words and actions at the time that his hand was with theirs on the Table. "If you are to be my disciples, the dominant motif of life must be servanthood," he said. "Life for others must be your way. No more yours the question of who shall be chief among you or who first in the kingdom; only, how do I act as a servant?" and those whom Jesus has confronted ever since are faced with the same choice.

The second meaning is that even after that choice is once made, with deep seriousness and full commitment, even after we have determined a life direction and a servant stance, the tension is not removed. We do not live in a world of absolutes, but in a world of relativities. There are no simple black and white decisions. We are part of a social structure where servanthood is no easy matter. Responsibilities exist on different levels for the man who is husband, father, wage-earner, and supervisor of a work force, to say nothing of his membership in the church, his status as a voter, consumer, and learner. You have made a commitment to servanthood as the dominant style of your life and you are at the same time a public school teacher, wife, mother, and church schoolteacher, to say nothing again of being at the same time a voter, consumer, home-owner, and investor. Other choices have continually to be made, compromises sought, best solutions determined out of many possible ones, none of which is perfect. That's the way our life is, even when we have made a fundamental choice about its primary direction, meaning, and purpose. We are always torn by the fundamental forces and powers in our lives and driven again and again to a re-examination of the

Lent 2: His Hand with Mine on the Table

Great Decision and weighing over and over the relativities of the lesser ones.

That's what happens at the Table. There the Suffering Servant confronts his disciples, and those who are considering discipleship, with the fundamental choice as to life's dominant motif—whether or not it will be the servant stance for us. The crisis of his decision is reconstituted in this room, his hand with ours on this table, his life calling ours to the way of servanthood. We are reminded of our decisions once before declared and given the opportunity to deepen our understanding of that way and our devotion to it. And it is brought home to us again that we are finite; children of God, but not God. We bring our halting and human thoughts and deeds before the judgment of One who suffered in all points like as we are and they are revealed for what they are. But, wonder of wonders, we are not condemned; we are loved and forgiven and made new. Our particular servanthood is clarified, strength to do our work is bestowed, and hope is revived.

Lent 3: In Anguish of Spirit He Prayed

Eugene Kidder and Robert A. Thomas

Thomas: The records of the closing days of Jesus' life, both by the amount of the material and the attention to detail, show how important the passion narrative was for the first Christians. Yet there are differences, both in emphasis and substance, between the four accounts which must be placed in proper perspective. The first Christians had no New Testament; they had only the Old Testament Scriptures, familiar to Jews but certainly not well-known to most first-century gentile Christians. The writings preserved in the New Testament were produced by the life of the church—out of its teaching and preaching, its theological and ethical controversies, its developing life of worship. And the first elements in the first collections were the preacher-accounts of the suffering, death, and resurrection of Jesus.

These first proclamations of the gospel, the good news of God, naturally varied. How could it be otherwise? Even eyewitnesses of events, close at hand and intimately involved, see happenings from different perspectives. Preachers and teachers have always freely selected and emphasized those factors in an experience that seem to them to most clearly make the point they are proclaiming. That kind of "fluid proclamation"

Lent 3: In Anguish of Spirit He Prayed

of the good news went on for decades before much was written down and before the various traditions and interpretations were fully crystallized in the Gospels which became Scripture.

The letters of Paul were written before the Gospels were composed, and other parts of the New Testament were completed before the Gospels were well-known or canonized as Scripture. All of this is important in connection with the parts of the passion narrative we have chosen to examine in this series of sermons and is particularly relevant to the story of the Gethsemane experience.

At the beginning of a chapter called "Gethsemane: The Great Tragedy," Joseph Klausner writes movingly of the last supper of Jesus with his friends, describing the misunderstandings and fears of the disciples, the enmity that had been stirred up among Jewish leaders, and the depression and dread of Jesus. And then he says: "The tragedy opened. Jesus went away to a garden called Gethsemane." That great Jewish scholar closes his examination of the event with these words:

> The whole story bears the hallmark of human truth: only a few details are dubious. It must have been transmitted to the Evangelists (or their sources) direct from Peter, James, or John, with such simplicity and conviction that even the ideas or tendencies of Pauline times could not obscure their memories. The sorrow and sufferings of the solitary Son of man, profound as they are, leave on every sympathetic heart, be it the heart of the believer or unbeliever, such an impression as may never be wiped out.[1]

Scarcely any part of the Bible is better known by Christians than the story of Jesus' praying in the garden the night of his arrest. Yet the question of the meaning of that event is far from settled, and that is partly true because of the different ways in which the New Testament authors deal with it. They deal with it in different ways because they saw Jesus from different perspectives, and all of them were describing the event on this side of calvary

---

1. Klausner, *Jesus of Nazareth*, 332.

and resurrection. Their tendency was surely to play down any indication of doubt, question, or uncertainty. (John doesn't even tell the story! It doesn't fit his theory about how a divine being would have acted.) None of them make it quite as strong as the author of Hebrews, who wrote before the tradition became fully crystallized and the gospel canonized as Scripture.

> In the days of his earthly life, he offered up prayers and petitions, with loud cries and tears, to God who was able to deliver him from the grave. Because of his humble submission his prayer was heard: son though he was, he learned obedience in the school of suffering, and once perfected, became the source of eternal salvation for all who obey him. (Heb 5:7–10 NEB)

The humanness of "loud cries and tears," "prayers and supplication" is unparalleled in the New Testament in its intensity. As Alexander Purdy writes, "the author had no inhibitions whatever in going the full length of equating Jesus' agony with the uttermost depth of human despair."[2] It was not that he had a "low" view of Jesus; it was rather that he did not shrink from identifying his "high" view with the fully human, deeply tragic experiences of life. Nor should we.

Kidder: Luke tells us in his terse way that after the supper Jesus "went out and made his way as usual to the Mount of Olives, accompanied by his disciples." That word "usual" alerts us that this was no magic garden of the gods, reserved for esoteric experience or a superhuman show of power. This place called Gethsemane, meaning "oil press," was associated with the squeezing out of the rich oils used for the anointing of kings. Perhaps this setting held for Jesus fond reminders of the high call to mission as well as the high cost. Here he may have labored his words again and again with his disciples, trying to help them see the real point of it all. Here may have been borne the constant misunderstandings of his message, the frequent wounds in the life of their intimate community, the

---

2. Purdy, "Hebrews" in Buttrick et al., *Interpreter's Bible*, vol. 11, 644.

Lent 3: In Anguish of Spirit He Prayed

many discouragements of their common effort to announce abroad the reality of God that was in them. All the while Jesus must have sensed he was fashioning from the human fiber of his disciples' lives a garment which could be worn again and again, a mantle of faith and leadership.

Gethsemane was holy ground, holy as are places about this community where the greatest triumphs of our mission have been celebrated and where the deepest of our sorrows have been shared. In these places we stand face to face with those who have known us as we are, not only to tell success or grieve loss as the common lot of all men, but to do so in the presence of the God of history. In this light the setting forth of the true human strength of men is a victory for all mankind and the terrible defeats are a cosmic groaning and the travail of the whole creation. Gethsemane closes the door on any spiritualizing of Jesus or of our faith in him. No more human picture of him is found in the New Testament. The valiancy in his work of mission and the agony of his suffering were so bound together in Jesus as to be almost indistinguishable. In Gethsemane these realities were expanded to ultimate proportions and Jesus was stretched to the breaking point. That event, written upon the face of history, epitomizes the deepest suffering of all who live in the spirit.

Jesus' power and leadership, measured in triumphal entries, is equally measured in agony. Maurice Goguel, writing of the life of Jesus, pictures him leaving the upper room to go to the Mount of Olives, "his mind . . . obsessed by the thought of the dangers which menaced him, and his trouble . . . increased by the feeling that he could not be absolutely certain of the loyalty of his disciples."[3] He has so deeply penetrated the meanings of life that men have come close in order to see what he sees. But he remains alone in his grasp of truth, much weightier in his apprehension of the gravity of the whole situation. So he walks forth, bent sharply upon the path he has always walked, now with a painful urgency, now more fully

---

3. Goguel, *Jesus and the Origins of Christianity*, 483.

aware that the great test of strength is very close. He walks out in patient strides, but swirling about his legs are not the gusts of glory but the dead winds of ominous defeat.

Two matters trouble him deeply. He has seen in the disciples their magnificent potential. He has watched the power of change at work in their lives, the sure announcement of a kingdom of the spirit that can alter the life of the world. His own certainty has been magnified. But now he has seen them when the chips are down. He has sat at table with them as they fussed over power, became absorbed in a fearful distrust of the reality they have known best, and are now panicked for their very life. Mark has Jesus, as he walks forth, speaking grimly, "You will all fall away," and to Peter "this very night, before the cock crows twice, you will deny me three times" (Mark 14:27, 30 RSV). From the vistas of his full faith in God, Jesus can see more than they themselves; the terror of the disciples and their weakness to withstand it. Thus doubt spills out of faith, for in the face of faith, doubt can be seen for what it is. And although this material in Mark may be included in the narrative in order to indicate the fulfillment of prophecy, it must mean to us that a real trial of spirit was underway with his disciples quite before Jesus' legal trials to follow.

Thomas: Nor did he escape grave doubts himself. This was the second of the great troubles to accompany him on his walk to the garden. He can go remembering the teaching which he has shared with the disciples and with many others. He can recall great works of healing which have built strength into the mission until its confidence is like a rock. He can call upon the endless resources of the grace of God which have been delivered to him in countless confrontations with earnest friends and frightened enemies. He goes now to his death as Frederick Grant says, "the ideal martyr . . . with soul prepared, his loins girt for the struggle, the 'athlete' of God utterly obedient to the Father's will, wholly consecrated for his ordeal."[4] It is this much preparation which can accept that much suffering!

4. Grant, "Mark," in Buttrick et al., *Interpreter's Bible*, vol. 7, 881.

Lent 3: In Anguish of Spirit He Prayed

No portion escapes him. Mark has it that he became "greatly distressed and troubled" (Mark 14:33), or in the Moffat translation "appalled and agitated." That he was facing costs he had not realized before was coming home. The terrors of physical sufferings were imminent. He saw now what he had not seen before, that his own likely destruction also meant the defeat of his mission, though not an incontrovertible one. So he began to mourn for the failure of the disciples, the loss of his own life, the loss of the mission by all human standards. His condition can best be described for our times as "deathly sick," or "so that he wished to die."

Kidder: The words of Luke are powerful enough, "In anguish of spirit he prayed the more urgently." He could wonder now, even in the face of astounding events of ministry, how he could ever have dared presume his word right over that of others, especially the religious leaders. With this powerful tension of strength and suffering, he stood in the tradition of the prophet Elijah, who though having found deep confidence in Yahweh through his encounter with the prophets of Baal, who often spoke how he was "very jealous for the Lord, the God of hosts," yet sat under a broom tree in the wilderness and "asked that he might die, saying, 'It is enough; now, O Lord, take away my life; for I am no better than my fathers'" (1 Kgs 19:4). The same tradition with the same polarity of forces occurs in Martin Luther, who, after his grand declaration before the Diet of Worms, sits in exile in Wartburg Castle asking: "Are you alone wise? Have so many centuries gone wrong? What if you are in error and are taking so many others with you to eternal damnation?" In the morning he threw open the casement window and looked out on the fair Thuringian hills. In the distance he could see a cloud of smoke rising from the pits of the charcoal burners. A gust of wind lifted and dissipated the cloud. Even so were his doubts dispelled and his faith restored."[5]

For Jesus the cup was suffering. Its symbolical significance is all that remains of the Gethsemane story in John. "Shall

---

5. Bainton, *Here I Stand*, 194.

I not drink the cup which the father has given me?" (John 18:11). Jesus' discovery of strength has come because of his willingness to walk directly into the midst of the worst threat to life. He has swallowed chaos and death not to be a poisoned Mr. Hyde, but rather to absorb their powers into the strength of redemption. The desperate agony required is not taken in any wish for delicious misery. Jesus loved life! and took on the terrible burdens only because they meant life. He longed that the whole matter could be spared for both his disciples and himself, but the ultimate and enduring nature of his mission provided him no escape.

Thomas: In his announcement to his disciples concerning their apostasy Jesus included a reminder of the enduring hope: "Nevertheless, after I am raised again I will go on before you into Galilee." Goodspeed describes Jesus as "downcast and apprehensive" upon leaving the city. Despair and dread crowd in upon him, yet prayer is what supports him. It gives him strength in his anguish and remains when all else is gone.

Kidder: Gethsemane leads not to enmity, but to sweat and tears of another kind. Jesus must have experienced an expanding compassion, seeing the terrible loss of life before him. He mourned too for his own helplessness, the shrinking of his own vision, taking place because in the nature of it there could be no fulfillment without those others for whom the Father cared. Such is the experience of any real spiritual leader, who under persecution knows that it is not himself but the spirit which he embodies that is under attack. Yet the forces of darkness sense that to destroy that spirit they must also destroy the man. Then comes the moment of exile in the spiritual pilgrimage. It is represented in Jesus' solitary retreat to a place alone, where time stands still. Utterly flattened by the onslaught, he takes complete leave of himself. It is like the strange experience when some deep loss has numbed us. Then as reality returns, the spirit seems to re-enter the body to once again address the grim task or the glorious hope.

Lent 3: In Anguish of Spirit He Prayed

Thomas: One does not think of the experience of Jesus apart from the reactions of the disciples. At every point in his life we are concerned with event and response, word and response. That is because we claim discipleship and we see ourselves in those responses of long ago. The poignancy of the passion narrative, the sense of the tragic which is there in spite of the resurrection faith, strikes us almost like a blow. Last Sunday we felt what it was to be with him at the Supper, "his hand with ours on the table." This morning we have thought of his agony and loneliness, his decision and his anguished prayer. But the haunting figures of the sleeping disciples, too tired or unaware to watch with him, come again and again to the fore. And we know what that means, too. Where were the others? One was on the way to betray him; the whereabouts of the rest we do not know. Scattered by fear? Watching from far off? Standing on the edge of the crowd of soldiers and officers who came to arrest him? Was hope gone yet? Did they still expect the miracle—the sudden rending of skies and coming of the hosts of God to set the messianic king on his throne? No one can say; only that they misunderstood who he was and the nature of his mission; only that they failed him when he needed them most.

Kidder: But that is not all there is to say about them. Those same men returned to the upper room and experienced the resurrection. They first proclaimed the good news. They carried the gospel across land and sea. They organized the church. They thought through the problems of the new faith in relationship to the old Israel. They produced the Scriptures. They "turned the world upside down."

Thomas: The meaning of the suffering got through to them. The God in whose presence and being he lived became their God. The Spirit he promised they were able to receive. The mission he began, they were able to carry on. So anguish may turn to acceptance, and failure of discipleship may be the prelude to commitment, and the purposes of God redeemed from the worst work of the enemies of the Son of Man.

Lent 4: His Teaching Is Causing Dissatisfaction

Thomas R. McCormick and Robert A. Thomas

Thomas: The accounts of the trials of Jesus before the religious and political authorities contain variations which reflect the several traditions represented in the New Testament. These variations have been the subject of endless scholarly research and a great deal of not-so-scholarly debate by less learned men. The sequence of events which most of us have learned is a composite of the materials of the four Gospels, but there is no way of being sure of the exact events.

Following the arrest in the garden of Gethsemane Jesus was taken before the Sanhedrin, the Jewish court of justice. The hereditary high priest was its head, and seventy other men—mostly Sadducees but at the time of Herod some Pharisees, too—composed the council. It exercised civil jurisdiction over all Jewish communities wherever they existed, but communities outside Judea regarded its authority less highly than those in Judea proper. One could think of it as the supreme court of their own people as contrasted with the foreign authority of Rome. It handled a variety of kinds of cases, but its primary responsibility had to do with questions connected with the Mosaic Law. It had its own officers and the right to arrest people, and it had authority to finally dispose of such cases as did not involve the sentence of death.

McCormick: According to the order in the Gospel of Mark, when Jesus was brought before this body the chief priests and all the members made vain attempts to find evidence on which they could convict him of some crime; witnesses appeared, but their evidence did not agree. They reported that they heard Jesus say, "I will destroy this Temple that is made with hands, and within three days I will build another made without hands." The high priest asked Jesus whether he had any reply to make to the charges, but Jesus made no answer. And then the high priest gave a new turn to the investigation by asking Jesus whether he was the Messiah, "the Son of the Blessed One," and Jesus replied, "I am, and you will see the Son of Man seated on the right hand of God and coming with the clouds of heaven."

Thomas: The answer is entirely characteristic of Jesus. The high priest's challenge had been put to him more than once earlier in his career and there is no reason to think he would have turned from a positive expression of his conviction at such a crucial point. To the high priest the answer was sheer blasphemy—a Galilean carpenter styling himself "Son of Man" in the sense of the book of Daniel. He tore his robes, the custom of a judge who heard blasphemous words, and turning to the members of the Sanhedrin asked, "'Need we call further witnesses? You have heard the blasphemy. What is your opinion?' Their judgment was unanimous that he was guilty and should be put to death" (Mark 14:63–64).

The narrative in Matthew differs in only a few points, but Luke's account, which we heard this morning, seems at first to be very different. The conclusion is the same; the Council judged him worthy of death. Mark and Matthew both report that after the Sanhedrin's adjournment Jesus was mocked and spit upon and struck, before being led, in the morning, to Pilate. Representatives of the Sanhedrin opened their case against him by suggesting that Jesus had subverted the nation, opposed payment of taxes to Caesar, and claimed to be Messiah, a king. The Roman governor asked him directly, "Are you the king of the Jews?" And Jesus replied, "The words are yours" (Luke 23:2–3). Again the answer was characteristic of Jesus: brief, pointed, enigmatic. As Klausner puts it, "What else could he answer to the foreign tyrant? He said not the least word more and this silence astonished Pilate."[1] He could find no fault with Jesus, but the crowd insisted, "His teaching is causing disaffection among the people all through Judea. It started from Galilee and has spread as far as this city" (Luke 23:5).

McCormick: Pilate then sent Jesus to Herod Antipas, the tetrarch of Galilee, under whose jurisdiction Jesus' case logically fell. Herod was in Jerusalem for the festival and was glad to have a chance to see the one who had become so famous for his miracles. But Herod could get nothing out of him (least of all the excitement of a miracle) and all Luke says is that Herod's soldiers treated Jesus with contempt and ridicule and sent him back to Pilate dressed in a "gorgeous robe" (Luke 23:11).

Pilate called the Sanhedrin together again, and once more indicated that he could find no facts to support their charges and neither could Herod, so proposed letting Jesus off with a flogging. But there was a general outcry, the crowd demanding the release of Barabbas and the crucifixion of Jesus. "Their shouts prevailed," Luke has it, "and Pilate decided they should have their way" (Luke 23:24).

Thomas: It is probable that the stories of Pilate's opposition to the crucifixion are unhistorical, particularly the public washing of hands, as Klausner and many Christian scholars believe; that they come from the end of the first century when large numbers of Gentiles had embraced Christianity and it had become clear that the future of Christianity depended upon the Gentiles and not the Jews, "who remained steadfast in their unbelief." The Roman Empire was then all-powerful and it was not politic to irritate it. The Jews were feeble, poor,

---

1. Klausner, *Jesus of Nazareth*, 346.

and persecuted. All we learn of Pilate from the writings of Josephus and Philo proves he was a "man of blood," cruel and tyrannical, to whom killing a single Galilean Jew was no more than killing a fly, a man who was always willing to provoke the Jews in every possible way.[2]

Whatever judgment one makes about the historicity of specific parts of the account of the trial of Jesus, or the responsibility one assigns to Jewish or Roman leaders for the decision to execute him, there can be no doubt that the word in Luke sums up the feeling of both groups: "His teaching is causing disaffection among the people all through Judea. It started from Galilee and has spread as far as this city" (Luke 23:5). Disaffection is a strong word, describing a condition that autocrats in every age and place fear. It means an alienation from those in authority; at least a lack of affection or good will; at most a tendency toward hostility and ill will. From the point of view of those interested in protecting the status quo, maintaining the establishment, carrying on in the traditional ways, the disaffected are disloyal and apt to be dangerous or traitorous. They are the dangerous nonconformists who must be silenced or destroyed.

McCormick: The charge of the Sanhedrin against Jesus deserves closer examination. They claimed, "his teaching is causing disaffection." Members of the Jewish nation who held positions of power and privilege under Roman rule had nothing to gain and much to lose in the event of an insurrection against Rome. On several occasions, with disastrous results, zealots and revolutionaries had attempted the impossible mission of driving out the Roman occupation troops. With the exception of the Maccabean rebellion, they all failed, and each time more freedom and opportunities for self-determination were lost. Jesus posed a real threat to the security of the chief Jewish rulers to the degree that he entertained any ambitions about a political or military revolution. And from a superficial point of view there was plenty of evidence that either he or his disciples

---

2. Klausner, *Jesus of Nazareth*, 348.

entertained such ambitions. Thus, in the words of Caiaphas the high priest, "It is expedient that one man should die."

Thomas: It is even clearer that another factor in the disaffection created by Jesus' teaching related to the ancient and elaborate legal system of Judaism. The Law had served the nomadic people at a stage in their life when clarity and discipline were important. But the life of the nation had radically changed over the centuries as they became a settled agricultural people, while their religious system carried the cultural hangovers from an all-but-forgotten day. The freedom which Jesus felt in his life, his concern for the existential moment, his high regard for persons above his regard for the law, all contributed to the disaffection about which the Sanhedrin now complained.

It is ever thus, the Word of God made Flesh creates disaffection in every time and place when things are valued over persons, when tyranny impinges on freedom, when ruthlessness replaces compassion, when someone forgets his brother or his neighbor. The disaffection will be felt in political realms which would hold themselves aloof from the prophetic call to social justice, or in congregations or persons who have not had ears to hear.

McCormick: As one analyzes the Scriptures which describe the life and teachings of Jesus, it becomes less certain that he made open messianic claims for himself, and more probable that his disciples and the writers of Scripture responded to his clear and decisive leadership by making these claims on his behalf. Especially, when looking in retrospect, the meaning of his life among them and the dramatic last events began to emerge in their thinking with a new and sharper clarity.

It is evident that in Jesus' response to the being and presence of God in his life, his commitment to the centrality of love, and his effort to make love real in deed, we meet the claim and the secret of his mission. Whether he is proclaiming the presence and coming of the kingdom of God or confronting the legalistic ethical judgment of the religious leaders of his day, his words and deeds stand in stark contrast to the

Lent 4: His Teaching Is Causing Dissatisfaction

accepted thought patterns of official religion. His personal gifts and leadership make him popular among the common people. His challenge of accepted concepts and codes aroused the suspicion of the chief priests and the Pharisees and Sadducees. Wherever he went he was confronted by the appeals of the sick, the hopes of his disciples, and the fears of his opposition. His betrayal by one of the twelve, the persistent denial of discipleship by another, his arrest, and finally his crucifixion are all a reply or a response from persons who encountered in his life and being certain forces which conflicted with all that they held dear and precious.

Thomas: Jesus said: "You have learned that they were told, 'an eye for an eye, and a tooth for a tooth.' But what I tell you is this: Do not set yourself against the man who wrongs you. You have learned that they were told, 'Love your neighbor, hate your enemy.' But what I tell you is this: Love your enemies and pray for your persecutors; only so can you be children of your heavenly Father, who makes his sun rise on good and bad alike, and sends the rain on the honest and dishonest" (Matt 5:38–43). Matthew says in an editorial comment, "When Jesus had finished this discourse the people were astounded at his teaching; unlike their own teachers he taught with a note of authority" (Matt 7:28).

McCormick: It was at this very point that Jesus' teachings came under the scrutiny of the religious officials, arousing their suspicions and fears, and finally enraging them to the point of seeking his quick destruction. His authority was accepted by the common people. His courageous integrity compelled him to speak in defiance of a legalistic way of life, and he was quick to blast out against the publicly pious preservers of "culture religion." These men were quickly able to recognize that if his teaching continued, and gained popular acceptance, the whole structure of Judaism would be undercut. They were not stupid nor wickedly perverse. Yet the forces of death were at work in their minds and hearts. There is every evidence that they were soon convinced that his death must come for the cause of God and Israel.

A classical illustration of the confusion between ceremonial piety and true religion is seen in the situation in which the angry crowd of Jewish religious leaders and officials gathered outside the praetorium (where Jesus was brought before Pilate) with death in their minds. Their hearts were set on his execution. Yet they were unwilling to step into the praetorium, thus defiling themselves ceremonially, and becoming ineligible for worship in the synagogue on the Sabbath Day. Here we see the striking contrast between man's fastidiousness in religious ceremony which is completely devoid of the spirit of loving acceptance for those whose style and view of life differ from their own, and the genuine spirit of self-giving love exemplified in the one standing quietly before Pilate.

Soren Kierkegaard reminds us that "truth lies in personal appropriation, not in man's intellectual furniture, but in the transformation of himself. Its characteristic is not that it is the same for all men at all times, but that it has power over one man's existence here and now. It is not in the dry light of reason, but in the warm heart, the passion for infinity, the unquenchable search and thirst for God that truth is won."[3]

Thomas: Thus, man's quest for God in every age has been threatened by diversion and perversion from the essential spirit, frequently in the name of true religion. Those today who abhor violence, who fear conflict, who oppose change, and who strive at all costs to keep intact "the American way of life" may thank God that it was not their fate to have lived in Jerusalem in AD 29, as Morton Enslin has said.[4]

McCormick: In every age, even our own, one of the chief obstacles to comprehending the greatness and the redemptive power of the Christian faith is the confusion between legalism and true religion; between issues of cultural pietism and the essential nature of Christianity. The tragedy of this is most evident

3. Allen, *Kierkegaard: His Life and Thought*, 146.
4. Enslin, *The Prophet from Nazareth*, 191.

Lent 4: His Teaching Is Causing Dissatisfaction

when a "legalistic hang-up" on social conventions like smoking, drinking, or swearing prevents one from participation in a redemptive, reconciling engagement with his fellow man. However, the forces of darkness are never left undisturbed by the brooding spirit of God. Not in Jerusalem, nor in Indianapolis, nor in Seattle. Settings which know conflict and change become scenes in which the persistent, redemptive, creative love of God is made known in the reality of human relationships, overcoming estrangement and alienation in the lives of men and women. The power of God, his love, his light, co-exists in this world with the forces of darkness and death. Wherever they meet, there has always been, and there is now, the disaffection which resulted from the teaching ministry of Jesus Christ.

Christopher Frye describes Greek tragedy as the catastrophe which occurs when the individual's vision or value conflicts with the structures of society. We have an example of it in the life of Socrates. We see it again in the death of Jesus. At that time, in the eyes of Pilate, Jesus could hardly have been seen much more seriously than Barabbas. The importance of dealing with conflict ensuing over his arrest by the Jewish officials was probably of no more consequence to him than the controversy with the Jews when he attempted to build an aqueduct carrying fresh water into Jerusalem employing funds which had been stored in the temple; or the crisis that was solved by removing his shields bearing the banner of Caesar from Jerusalem to Caesaria. Yet, history has given meaning to this event, and the tragedy of this man's struggle has given birth to courage in the hearts of men in every age. In our own time we might point to the growing number of young men in our nation whose sense of moral value and whose conscience will not allow them to fight a war in Vietnam, and thus find themselves in conflict with the value systems and structures of society and subject to long terms in prison.

The political revolutions which have toppled autocratic governments all over the world serve to remind us that the freeing spirit which affirms the worth of the individual can be dangerous to the status quo. The kind of social autocracy which for too long has emasculated the lives of men whose skin is various shades of black or brown cannot last forever. The kind of religion, or any other structure, which seeks to manipulate man for its own ends, making him a thing instead of a person, will find the seeds of disaffection sown when the spirit of God brings truth to light.

Thomas: Part of the tragic element in the whole "Christ-event" is the revealing it brings of the evil tendencies in human nature and human institutions. We are brought up short when we think that the "Man for Others" is condemned by both religious and political leaders, because "his teaching causes disaffection." One would think that commitment to the value of human life, to the freeing of persons to be fully human, to the needs of the most distressed and troubled men, would surely result in the applause and appreciation of the leaders of both religious and political institutions. But Pilate sends Jesus off to horrible death, and that tragic low regard for the worth of human life is not a drama which has played its final scene. That system of values which puts the structures of institutions ahead of the worth of persons, that exalts the material as more important than the personal, that refuses to hear the Word of life and acknowledge the presence of Christ in the call of the dispossessed, still sees serious disciples of Christ as those who are causing disaffection.

One of the reasons for the struggles in the church of our time is the new insistence of its most committed leaders and members that the faith relate to the life of the world, that the church speak and act as its Lord, that it really become a servant people, that it turn from its temptation to accept the judgments of the world about its life and work and test its life and work by the revealing Word of God alone. And that determination brings the institution face to face with its phony forms, its empty fellowship, its superficial worship, its pious phrases, and its determination to extend itself even at the expense of a forthright proclamation of the gospel.

Lent 4: His Teaching Is Causing Dissatisfaction

The teaching of Jesus caused disaffection throughout Galilee and Judea in the days of his earthly life. It has been causing disaffection ever since, and so it will continue—until the kingdom comes. Every legalistic institution, every kind of autocracy—political, religious, or social—is finally doomed by that word: "His teaching is causing disaffection."

Lent 5: Do Not Weep for Me, Weep for Yourselves and Your Children

Robert A. Thomas

Our concern in this Lenten series has been to speak of "his life" and "our life"; to discover in the major events in the last period of Jesus' life the meanings that are significant for our time in the world's history. We have become more aware of the tragic element in all of life, of the background of circumstances and the inner tensions and fears that to a great degree chart the course of events. We have faced head-on the difficult and controversial question of New Testament scholarship so as to make clear the reality of events which have been covered over with layers of tradition and thereby lost not only their original meaning but also their touch with our human condition.

We are as convinced as the Jesuit poet Daniel Berrigan that the meaning of being a Christian needs to be redefined in every age, and we agree with him that "every age hesitates between two great choices: that of insecurity, in the world and that of a security which merely draws on what has gone before, and remains on safe ground. The real effort, never really done with, is to discern what Christ is saying to us from within the real world . . . all else is a mortician's job or a child's game."[1]

---

1 Berrigan, "Fidelity to the Living: Reflections," in Marty and Peerman, *New Theology: No. 3*, 179–80.

Lent 5: Do Not Weep for Me, Weep for Yourselves and Your Children

We have been working hard and seriously at the task of redefinition and we do not think we have been playing games or engaged in embalming a corpse! Our commitment is to the Living God, made known in the Christ-event; not only in an age long past, but in this nation now. As in every city in the nation this spring there is apprehension among us. The crisis of our separations looms ahead and there is "no hiding place down there." Every public meeting takes some notice of the situation, and so does every newscast and issue of the daily papers. Though many agencies and persons in our community have stepped up programs and activities to meet the pressing problems, there is growing evidence of frustration. There is lack of leadership to foster change and unwillingness on the part of the majority to make the sacrifices necessary to the achievement of justice. The tragic consequences of these conditions are about to break upon us, even when there is a great reservoir of good will, desire to help, and awareness of the impending judgment.

It is in this kind of world, where the skein of tragedy is woven through the texture of human life, that we have to measure the meaning and significance of Jesus' life, answer the questions about the nature of the Ultimate Reality, and make the fundamental choices and commitments regarding our own lives.

The primitive tradition of the death of Jesus was surely quite simple. It told how Jesus was taken to Golgotha and crucified after he had been offered some drugged wine according to the usual custom. A *titulus* was placed on the cross which made known that he had been condemned as King of the Jews; then the soldiers divided his garments among themselves. After a time of agony (comparatively short in terms of ordinary crucifixions) he died. Maurice Goguel thinks the first accounts were that simple and that the added sections which all the Gospels contain are reasonably easy to identify and explain. Other scholars basically agree, though all make allowances for the possibility of the historicity of the details which we have in the New Testament accounts.

Tradition records the last words of nearly all the great personalities of history. It is not surprising that persons who were present at the time of the crucifixion remembered some of what Jesus said; nor is it surprising that they remembered it in different ways and in different sequence. Nor would it be surprising that some words were remembered out of context, misunderstood, and perhaps misinterpreted. The author of Mark reports only one "saying from the cross," and the same word is reported in Matthew. But Luke reports three other sayings and John reports another three. Ethelbert Stauffer, New Testament professor at the University of Erlangen, Germany, tends to accept all the sayings from the cross as historical, though he believes they are quotations from the Psalms that have been mostly twisted and misunderstood in Christian tradition.

It is important for us to picture with reasonable accuracy the historical event, and we do have descriptions from extra-biblical sources of the common practices of the Romans. Crucifixion was an execution method of eastern origin, which came into general use by the Romans, particularly as a punishment for slaves. The Jewish historian, Josephus, says that it was often used in Palestine and that after the siege of Jerusalem Titus crucified so many Jews that "there was not room for the crosses, nor enough crosses for the condemned."[2] As in all the ancient world, executions were in public, generally near towns or cities and at cross-roads in the sight of all who passed by.

The shape of the crosses varied; sometimes merely a stake or tree to which the victim was fastened by his hands; sometimes in two parts, a post to which a crossbeam was attached, either at the top in the shape of a "T" or down the post as our normal way of picturing it. The one to be crucified customarily carried his own crossbeam to the execution grounds where the posts for the crosses already stood, left from former crucifixions. The condemned was stripped, fastened with cords or nails to the crossbeam and then the beam fastened or nailed in place, the cross just high enough to keep the feet from touching the ground. It was "the acme of the torturer's art," as Albert Reville describes it:

> Atrocious physical sufferings, length of torment, ignominy, the effect of the crowd gathered to witness the long agony of the crucified. Nothing could be more horrible than the sight of this living body, breathing, seeing, hearing, still able to feel, and yet reduced to the state of

---

2. Goguel, *Jesus and the Origins of Christianity*, 2:534.

Lent 5: Do Not Weep for Me, Weep for Yourselves and Your Children

a corpse by forced immobility and absolute helplessness. . . . It represented miserable humanity reduced to the last degree of impotence, suffering and degradation."[3]

Matthew and Mark both report that before Jesus was executed he was scourged. That means he was flogged with a whip of thongs, weighted at the ends with sharp metal or bone, capable of drawing blood at every blow. It was such a cruel punishment that sometimes victims died. Then Pilate sent his execution squad with the condemned man to a small hill called Golgotha outside the northwest wall of the city. I saw two sites in Jerusalem, each of which was described in absolute terms as the exact place of the crucifixion: one inside the Church of the Holy Sepulchre, a site fixed by Helena, mother of Constantine, about 325 AD by a special vision; the other out-of-doors near an open tomb called Gordon's Calvary. The truth is, no one can be sure of the site, nor does it make much difference.

Jesus was unable to carry the crossbeam all the way from Pilate's judgment hall to Golgotha, probably because of the effect of the scourging, and Luke reports that a man by the name of Simon from the North African city of Cyrene, who was on his way into Jerusalem, was seized by the Roman soldiers and pressed into carrying it for him. He also reports that "great numbers of people followed, many women among them, and that Jesus said to them, 'Daughters of Jerusalem, do not weep for me; no, weep for yourselves and your children'" (23:28). Joseph Klausner says that a very ancient rabbinical record reports that "when a man is going out to be killed they suffer him to drink a grain of frankincense in a cup of wine to deaden his senses . . . wealthy women of Jerusalem used to contribute these things and bring them."[4]

Not much is said about the crucifixion in Luke. Jesus was placed between two thieves, one of whom mocked him and one who asked for his help. They put an inscription on the cross beam

---

3. Réville, *Jésus De Nazareth*, 405, cited by Goguel, *Jesus and the Origins of Christianity*, 536. [These citations are garbled in the typescript and this rendition has not been confirmed.]

4. Klausner, *Jesus of Nazareth*, 332.

making it clear that he was crucified as "King-Messiah," another indication that Jesus had so declared himself. He may have hung from nine o'clock in the morning till three o'clock in the afternoon, though the tradition has accepted the shorter period from noon till three o'clock. Death by crucifixion generally took two days at least, often longer, and Jesus' death in a few hours is another indication that he was very feeble. The horrible physical sufferings were beyond the power of his endurance; the spiritual sufferings hardly less. Some of his women friends were there, and his mother. There may have been some disciples from Galilee, but the men had gone, afraid of being suspected as his followers. Nobody was concerned about women disciples; they hardly started revolutions.

Mark and Matthew both report what seems at first to be a terrible cry of dereliction just before Jesus died, "My God, my God, why hast thou forsaken me?" Bornkamm reminds us that "it is a cry of prayer—certainly not the cry of one who has despaired of God; and yet we must not take away from the harshness and depth of suffering expressed in the words."[5] It is surely an authentic word from the cross; for the early church could never have imagined that Jesus felt himself deserted by God. The first two evangelists felt bound to relate it, though Luke and John could not bear its striking contrast to Jesus' confident and perfect communion with the Father and they do not report it all.

The picture of his death is differently presented by Luke. As soon as the cross is set up, Jesus utters a prayer for his enemies. Then the penitent thief seeks Jesus' help and is assured of pardon and salvation. And finally come the words from Ps 31, "Father, into thy hands I commit my spirit."

According to John, before he dies he speaks three other words: commending his mother to the care of his favorite disciple, expressing his thirst, and finally saying, "It is finished." Bornkamm's judgment is that "these are three great, and in themselves profoundly different, pictures of the crucified. They must not be taken as fragments of a historical record, and then pieced together to make a

---

5. Bornkamm, *Jesus of Nazareth*, 166–76.

Lent 5: Do Not Weep for Me, Weep for Yourselves and Your Children

whole, however clearly all of them express, in their differences and despite their differences, the mystery of the person, mission, and death of Jesus."[6]

It is a most important fact to remember that the authors of the Gospels resisted the temptation to which I have almost succumbed this morning and that has trapped Christians through the ages. They did *not* attempt to emphasize the physical torture Jesus endured in the crucifixion; what they retained was a precise recollection of his spiritual agony, the sense of being abandoned by God. They did not seek pity for Jesus and made it clear he did not seek it for himself.

Erik Routley writes that our response to the crucifixion should be a complex of emotions ranging from shame to joy, but that pity is excluded by the words in Luke that are the title of this morning's sermon. Jesus said to the women of Jerusalem, those professional mourners who met the execution squad on the way to Golgotha, "Daughters of Jerusalem, do not weep for me; no, weep for yourselves and your children" (23:36). That saying rules out a number of our popular hymns and any number of the works of poets of devotion whose attempt is to evoke pity in their hearers or singers; not "I had a hand in this" but rather, "How wicked were those who did this to him."[7] It suggests that the famous section in Stainer's "The Crucifixion," "Is it nothing to you, all ye that pass by? Behold, and see if there be any sorrow like unto my sorrow" is phony. Applying that verse from Lamentations (1:12) to Jesus is not legitimate; for self-pity was foreign to his nature. His concern was for the others, and his solicitude for the women of Jerusalem, as well as for his mother and his women disciples from Galilee, bears witness to a self-transcendence that rebukes and humbles us.

It was not his death that was the significant thing, but the rejection of his word, the refusal to respond to his mission. The women were but the representatives of all those whom he sought to enlist in his kingdom's cause but who turned away. They would

---

6. Bornkamm, *Jesus of Nazareth*, 167.
7. Routley, *The Man for Others*, 80.

not believe the "Day of the Lord" was at hand. They would not change from the pursuit of personal pleasure or material things or nationalistic glory in true repentance to the God of love and grace. Their materialism and legalism and selfish pride stood in the way—wealthy women, religious leaders, a rich young ruler, even disciples who had been with him for months and still missed the point of it all.

Translated into our own time: he does not need our pity; we need his love and encouragement. And the tragedy is that so many of us seem to have it backwards. We feel we are doing something for God when we feel sorry for Jesus; that pity for him is a truly significant religious emotion. God does not need our pity; we need his power. Jesus did not need or want the weeping of the women of Jerusalem; they needed what he had to give.

Did you see the picture of that little black boy on the cover of *Life* magazine a couple of weeks ago? He was crying for himself and for his people and for all of us. And that's the way it ought to be. We weep for ourselves; the men killing each other in Vietnam and Jordan; the fatherless children in the ghettos; the kids whose anger and rebelliousness bursts out in destructive looting; the businessmen whose shops are damaged; all of us who are citizens of this land of noble birth and high ideals watching its purposes betrayed. We weep for the women and children of Vietnam, north and south, and for the starving peasants of India, and for the statemen and diplomats who don't know the world has changed. We weep for those who think they possess the good life only to discover that living has passed them by. We weep for parents who try to dictate to their children and children whose emancipation is made impossible; for men and women who are so turned in on themselves that they are unable to reach out to others in love. We weep for all the destructiveness and inability to come to grips with reality that is around us. We weep not for him, but for ourselves and our children; for all the tragic limitations and failures that keep the world from becoming the kingdom of God's love.

Alfred North Whitehead suggests that as soon as high consciousness is reached in the human evolution, the enjoyment of existence is entwined with pain, frustration, loss, and tragedy, but

Lent 5: Do Not Weep for Me, Weep for Yourselves and Your Children

there is an element in our constitution that sees the tragedy as "a living agent persuading the world to aim at fitness beyond the faded level of surrounding fact. Each tragedy is the disclosure of an ideal; what might have been and was not: What can be. The tragedy is not in vain."[8]

---

8. Whitehead, *Adventures of Ideas*, 285.

Lent 6: Why Search Among the Dead for One Who Lives?

Robert A. Thomas

"Then Jesus gave a loud cry and died" (Mark 15:37). The tragic forces of misunderstanding and simple human error, fear of change and determination to maintain the status quo, love of power and pride in separatist traditions, legalistic attitudes toward the nature of truth and lack of awareness of God's creative word in the world had their way. The proclaimer of God's presence and love, the friend of sinners and tax-collectors, the prophet-messiah from Galilee, herald of a coming kingdom, was executed.

It is impossible to read that story, even knowing what we know of the sequel, even sharing what we share of history and present community of faith, without a deep sense of the awful depths of evil which permeate human existence. We have little appreciation of the reality of the gospel, of the meaning of the resurrection faith, without experiencing fully the fact of the tragic death of Jesus of Nazareth. He was crucified, having beforehand been flogged by men in places of power and judgment, men who had given (or who had won) the right to make judgments about the lives of others. In those acts we recognize the forces and powers that still exist in human life—in us—that seem indissolubly part of our human condition.

Lent 6: Why Search Among the Dead for One Who Lives?

We are grieved that his friends "had all been standing at a distance," and that the women who had come with him from Galilee "stood with them and watched it all." With a sense of relief one reads in Luke's account that one member of the Great Council of the Jews, a certain Joseph of Arimathea had withheld his vote to take the Nazarene before Pilate on the trumped-up charge of sedition and, in defiance of his colleagues and of public opinion, went to Pilate after Jesus' death and asked for the body to give it a decent burial. "Taking it down from the cross, he wrapped it in a linen shroud, and laid it in a tomb cut out of the rock, in which no one had been laid before. It was Friday, and the Sabbath was about to begin" (24:53–54).

But the "tragedy had an epilogue." It was not long before the disciples emerged from hiding, and the despair in which the crucifixion plunged them, to face the world in confidence and courage, rejoicing in a mighty faith and a new hope. That faith spread, living in the face of ridicule and opposition, persecution and violent death. It laid hold of multitudes and it effected the transformation of human hearts in such dramatic ways as to change the moral-spiritual climate of the world. Only one explanation seems adequate, that given by the author of Luke-Acts: "God raised him to life again, setting him free from the pangs of death, because it could not be that death should keep him in its grip" (Acts 2:24).

The only alternatives are to suppose that the Christian church and the Christian faith were based on illusion or on deliberate imposture; and while both of those alternatives have been suggested from the beginning, they have never been thought adequate by reasonable men of faith or no faith. The Jesus scholar, Joseph Klausner, wrote, "It is impossible to suppose that there was any conscious deception: the nineteen-hundred-years' faith of millions is not founded on deception."[1]

But how are people of our time, whose worldviews and ways of approach to the "facts" of human life are so far removed from those of the first century, to understand the resurrection? What is the meaning of the biblical faith? There is no escape for the serious

---

1. Klausner, *Jesus of Nazareth*, 359.

Christian from confronting this problem; for the resurrection is the cornerstone of the church's life. "What the early church felt was Jesus' presence with every Christian heart, all over the ancient world." That became and remained the fundamental conviction of the early church.[2] It was the experience of Paul, the inspirer of the stories of resurrection appearances in the Synoptic Gospels, the key to the Gospel of John, and the continuing faith of the church to this very moment of history.

What has to be said for us in this time, in view of the body of knowledge that is quite generally known and accepted, and in view of the inconsistencies and problems in the gospel record, is that *the resurrection faith must be distinguished from the Gospel stories about it*. Unless that is done it seems impossible and irrelevant for people in our time.

We had occasion more than once in the Lenten season to call attention to the fact that the biblical narratives in connection with the passion of Jesus are composed from different points of view, seeking to state the meaning of the events as the authors understood them so as to make a proclamation of the good news of God to the various audiences the authors had in mind. The Gospels are not "historical writing" as we understand this phrase. They need to be freed from a strict kind of literalist reading, characteristic of our grandfather's time, if their message is to be heard now.

The earliest account of the amazing sequel to the crucifixion of Jesus and the first despair of his disciples comes from the hand of Paul, who twenty-five years later wrote to the Corinthians about it. He had told them of it years before when he had first visited Corinth in 50 AD, and he thought of it as the most important thing he had to tell. Gunther Bornkamm regards it as the "old form" of the tradition, formulated long before Paul, and the most reliable Easter text:

> I handed on to you the facts which have been imparted to me: that Christ died for our sins, in accordance with the scriptures; that he was buried; that he was raised to life on the third day, according to the scriptures; and that

2. Goodspeed, *A Life of Jesus*, 226.

he appeared to Cephas, and afterwards to the Twelve. Then he appeared to over five hundred of our brothers at once, most of whom are still alive, though some have died. Then he appeared to James and afterwards to all the apostles. In the end he appeared even to me. . . . This is what we all proclaim, and this is what we believe." (1 Cor. 15:3–11)

That reads like an official record, but it mentions appearances that have no trace in the Gospels. There is nothing in that Pauline record of women at an empty tomb or disciples on the road to Emmaus. It says Peter was the first witness, the first to become conscious of the presence of Christ with him, but there is no record of that in the Gospels. Furthermore, that experience of Peter's is thought of in exactly the same terms Paul thought of his own experience on the Damascus road.

The evangelists do not agree among themselves nor with Paul. Mark and Matthew record appearances of Jesus in Galilee, while Luke and John have them entirely in Jerusalem. Paul begins with Peter's experience; the Gospels with the women who went to the tomb. Mark speaks of women who are afraid so that they told no one, but Luke has them tell the apostles "and all the others." The most important difference is the way in which the resurrection is conceived. We can't be sure what Mark thought, since the ending of his Gospel apparently was lost, but the other Gospel writers represent the appearances of Christ as corporeal, material, while Paul is clearly describing spiritual events.

What all these variations mean is simply that the resurrection tradition was in a fluid state longer than the tradition of the passion, allowing for more legendary accretions. The Easter message was earlier than the Easter stories, and faith in the presence of the Living Christ did not originally, nor does it now, depend upon the historicity of stories reporting a resurrection body of flesh and bones. The Risen Christ was visible only to the eye of faith; he was not seen by Pilate or Herod or members of the Jewish hierarchy, or by anyone who was blind and unresponsive to the truth in him.[3]

---

3. Tittle, *The Gospel According to Luke*, 268.

Paul proclaimed that Christ by his death opened a new life to those who accepted his gift. "The gift God gives is eternal life through union with Christ Jesus our Lord." Living means Christ. Christ is everything and in us all. He is our true life. In union with him we are all one. As Dr. Goodspeed wrote, "Paul, who had never seen or heard Jesus caught from him his great sense that religion was not a legislation, and could not be reduced to one, and also caught his great vision of the love of God and love for men, of which John afterward made so much."[4]

John began where Paul left off. Jesus has come back to trusting hearts as the Holy Spirit, the Comforter, the Helper, the Counselor, guiding them into the full truth. Apparently the idea that Jesus' resurrection was a physical re-animation played only a very brief role in the serious thinking of the ancient church; for John thought of his return as an inward, spiritual force that proved to be indomitable. "God loved the world so much that he gave his only Son, that everyone who has faith in him may not die but have eternal life" (John 3:16).

In another place John writes: "Dear friends, let us love one another, because love is from God. Everyone who loves is a child of God and knows God, but the unloving know nothing of God. For God is love; and his love was disclosed to us in this, that he sent his only Son into the world to bring us life" (1 John 4:7–9).

The most precious conviction of those early Christians was that they were "in Christ," united to him, in communion and communication with him. "Jesus opened up their way to God and they believed he was still their great companion." They knew him to be bread of life, water of life, light of the world who gave sight to the blind, healed the sick, raised the spiritually dead. He lighted the way to knowledge, truth, and freedom, "great words in the old Greek world and great words today."[5] God had not permitted Jesus to go down to defeat but had raised him up and given him glory! Nothing could separate them from the love of God manifest in Christ.

---

4. Goodspeed, *A Life of Jesus*, 227.

5. Goodspeed, *A Life of Jesus*, 227.

Lent 6: Why Search Among the Dead for One Who Lives?

Christ continued with his disciples as indwelling spirit and redeeming love and power. That was the actual experience of the first Christians and it has been the experience of Christians down through the ages. As the Jesuit poet Daniel Berrigan has written, it is nonsense to talk about what Jesus would do if he returned. "The Risen One has never departed. He has become a life-giving spirit. . . . Fidelity to the mystery means fidelity to the One who is present neither as memory nor image nor law, but as Event in all events, Man in all men, victory beyond all defeat, a continuing defeat and a delayed victory."[6]

One of the great modern historians of the church says there can be no doubt that Christians through the ages have been honest in reporting an experience of "being with a Presence" associated with the historical Jesus. People have been called from defeat and despair to triumphant hope. They have found the power to go through suffering, disappointment, and the loss of loved ones. They have found strength to engage in the battle against enthroned wrong and age-long evils; and yet to do so in humility; without vindictiveness and in love.[7]

Martin Luther King embodied that strength in a rare and wonderful way. He said in 1963: "I confess that I never intend to become adjusted to the evils of segregation and the crippling effects of discrimination, to the moral degeneracy of religious bigotry and the corroding effects of narrow sectarianism, to economic conditions that deprive men of work and food, and to the insanities of militarism and the self-defeating effects of physical violence."[8]

We come today to celebrate, in the mood of solemn rejoicing. We bear a testimony; we make a witness. We do not come to argue the faith, to try to prove anything; only to say that for us the Christ-event is the center of history; that the deepest meaning of existence has been revealed in the life of a Person whose Spirit continues to lead us into fullest truth. The forces of darkness and tragedy are real

---

6. Berrigan, "Fidelity to the Living: Reflections," in Marty and Peerman, *New Theology: No. 3*, 190.

7. Latourette, *Anno Domini*, 236–37.

8. *Time*, April 12, 1968, 20.

enough; they are responsible for a crucifixion, war, assassination, riot, burning, and destruction. But they do not have the last word!

Christianity at its best has not been greatly interested in proving anything about itself or the character of its mission in the world. It has announced a mystery: the divine gift, forgiveness, hope, eternal life. It has pointed to *signs*. It has celebrated God's presence and work in the creative process of the universe, in the love of people for their fellows, in the ministries of people of good will even in awful times. What we declare in this terrible time is that the emancipating event has occurred; that Christ has infinite significance both for the individual destiny and for the future of the human race.

The night of Dr. King's murder,[9] following some pictures of his marches, meetings, and addresses, NBC's "Chet Huntley tilted his head away from the camera, battled back tears and said: 'Again we are made to look like a nation of killers. Restraint, gentleness and charity, virtues we so desperately need, have had a dark day.'"[10]

Who has not asked this past ten days, "Does life have any abiding meaning? Does it participate in real being?" J. H. Oldham says in his little book, *Life Is Commitment*, that the more honestly and deeply we face the realities of human existence the clearer it becomes that we have nothing whatever to hope for in ourselves. "When we become alive to that reality, there is no refuge from despair, no truth in which our minds can rest, nothing that can give us back confidence and hope, except the knowledge that there is an undeserved mercy on which we can cast ourselves and an unmerited grace in which we can put our trust."[11]

That does not mean we have no responsibility for ourselves, no capacities for learning and growth, for hope and love and self-direction. That does not mean we can escape from the burdens of the world, from the tasks of civilization and building decent community life in which all can live as free and equal, and from full participation in the labors by which we through our knowledge

---

9. Martin Luther King Jr., was assassinated April 4, 1968. This sermon was preached on Easter Sunday, April 14, 1968. Robert F. Kennedy was assassinated on June 5 of that same year.

10. *Time*, April 12, 1968, 82.

11. Oldham, *Life Is Commitment*, 83.

and industry make ourselves masters of our environment. It does mean that in the end there is nothing to cling to except the belief that there is a love which accepts us just as we are and will do for us more than we can ask or think. It does mean that beyond the mountaintop is the promised land.

Many today stand dismayed at the gulf that separates the man of Galilee from the people of this age. The comfortable old beliefs by which they have sought to bridge that ever-widening gulf have been taken away. Like Mary Magdalene and those other women, they come in sorrow to shed a final tear over him, to make their farewells. The years have taken him away and they know not where he has been laid. But the word of the gospel is, "Why do you search among the dead for one who lives?"

That is our faith; that is our testimony this Easter day. We are not alone in an uncaring universe—alone with our sins and follies, our loss and grief and pain, our guns with telescopic sights, our unbridled hates and unreasonable judgments, our racism and nuclear power, our divided church with its traditional forms and reluctance to serve in the world. We are in the hands of God and God is the One "who raised Christ Jesus from the dead."

Bibliography

Allen, E. L. *Kierkegaard: His Life and Thought*. New York: Harper, 1935.
Allen Jr., O. Wesley. *The Homiletic of All Believers: A Conversational Approach to Proclamation and Preaching*. Louisville: Westminster John Knox, 2005.
Allen, Ronald J., and O. Wesley Alllen Jr. *The Sermon Without End: A Conversational Approach to Preaching*. Nashville: Abingdon, 2015.
Bainton, Roland. *Here I Stand*. Nashville: Abingdon, 1950.
Bell, Charles G. "Tragedy." *Dialogues* 7 (June 1, 1954) 12–32.
Blake, Albert Edward. *The Gospel in Hymns: Backgrounds and Interpretations*. New York: Scribner, 1950.
Bornkamm, Gunther. *Jesus of Nazareth*. New York: Harper, 1960.
Buttrick, George A., et al., eds. *The Interpreter's Bible*. Vols. 7 and 11. Nashville: Abingdon, 1951.
Buttrick, George A., et al., eds. *The Interpreter's Dictionary of the Bible*. Vol. 3. Nashville: Abingdon, 1964.
Carpenter, George Wayland. *Encounter of the Faiths*. New York: Friendship, 1967.
Enslin, Morton Scott. *The Prophet from Nazareth*. New York: McGraw Hill, 1961.
Gardner, John W. *Self-Renewal: The Individual and the Innovative Society*. New York: Harper & Row, 1963.
Goguel, Maurice. *Jesus and the Origins of Christianity*. Translated by Olive Wyon. Vol. 2, *The Life of Jesus*. New York: Harper, 1933.
Goodspeed, Edgar J. *A Life of Jesus*. New York: Harper, 1950.
Hammarskjöld, Dag. *Markings*. Translated by Leif Sjöberg and W. H. Auden. New York: Knopf, 1965.
Hiltner, Seward, and Lowell G. Colston. *The Context of Pastoral Counseling: A Comparative Study with Some Histories*. New York: Abingdon, 1961.
Hollinger, David A. *After Cloven Tongues of Fire: Protestant Liberalism in Modern American History*. Princeton: Princeton University Press, 2013.
Howe, Reuel L. *The Miracle of Dialogue*. New York: Seabury, 1963.

Bibliography

———. *Partners in Preaching: Clergy and Laity in Dialogue*. New York: Seabury, 1967.

James, William. *The Varieties of Religious Experience*. New York: Random House, 1902.

Killen, Patricia O'Connell, and Mark Silk, eds. *Religion and Public Life in the Pacific Northwest: The None Zone*. Religion by Region 1. Walnut Creek, CA: AltaMira, 2004.

Klausner, Joseph. *Jesus of Nazareth: His Life, Times, and Teaching*. Translated by Herbert Danby. New York: Macmillan, 1945.

Langer, Susanne K. *Philosophical Sketches: A Study of the Human Mind in Relation to Feeling, Explored Through Art, Language, and Symbol*. New York: Mentor, 1964.

Latourette, Kenneth Scott. *Anno Domini: Jesus, History, and God*. New York: Harper, 1935.

Macquarrie, John. *God and Secularity*. New Directions in Theology Today 3. Edited by William Hordern. Philadelphia: Westminster, 1967.

Marty, Martin E., and Dean G. Peerman. *New Theology, No. 3*. New York: Macmillan, 1966.

McClure, John S. *The Roundtable Pulpit: Where Leadership and Preaching Meet*. Nashville: Abingdon, 1995.

Nietzsche, Friedrich. *Thus Spoke Zarathustra*. Translated by Thomas Common. New York: Random House, 1962.

Oldham, J. H. *Life Is Commitment*. New York: Association, 1950.

Osborn, Ronald E. "A Functional Definition of Preaching: A Tool for Historical Investigation and Homiletical Criticism." *Encounter* 37, no. 1 (1976) 53–72.

———. *The Spirit of American Christianity*. New York: Harper, 1958.

Réville, Albert. *Jésus De Nazareth: Études Critiques Sur Les Antécédents De L'histoire Évangélique Et La Vie De Jésus*. 2 vols. 2nd ed. Paris: Libr. Fischbascher, 1906.

Routley, Erik. *The Man for Others*. New York: Oxford University Press, 1964.

Scott Jr., Nathan A. *The Tragic Vision and the Christian Faith*. New York: Association, 1957.

Thomas, Robert A. *A Sketch of the History of University Christian Church*. Seattle: University Christian Church, 1965.

Tittle, Ernest Fremont. *The Gospel According to Luke: Exposition and Application*. New York: Harper, 1951.

van der Geest, Hans. *Presence in the Pulpit: The Impact of Personality in Preaching*. Translated by Douglas W. Stott. Atlanta: John Knox, 1981.

Watkins, Keith. *Liturgies in a Time When Cities Burn*. Nashville: Abingdon, 1969.

Whitehead, Alfred North. *Adventures of Ideas*. New York: Mentor, 1955.

Wright, Frank Lloyd. *The Future of Architecture*. New York: Mentor, 1963.

www.ingramcontent.com/pod-product-compliance
Lightning Source LLC
Chambersburg PA
CBHW071442160426
43195CB00013B/2003